STOLEN

by Rebecca Petty

...And the day of vengeance of our God;
To comfort all who mourn,
To console those who mourn in Zion,
To give them beauty for ashes,
The oil of joy for mourning,
The garment of praise for the spirit of heaviness...

Isaiah 61:2-3 *(NKJ Version)*

Cover by Kristy Fricker

PROLOGUE
2019

Twenty years have passed since I last saw your face, held your hand, and heard your voice. So much has changed. I have changed. Sometimes, I think the world may be a crueler place than it was back in 1999, but then again, how could anything be crueler than what happened to you? I guess what I'm trying to say is that it is very different from when you were here. I'm not talking about the obvious changes like the explosion of social media or the rocky political climate. I mean things closer to home, like the fact that your middle sister has made you an aunt to children you will never know. How your nephew almost died when he was born because his lungs collapsed but is now a normal, healthy 9-year-old with Fort Nite and basketball on the brain. And your niece is the spitting image of you, with your looks and personality. Sometimes, her mother calls me and says, "I think I have given birth to the reincarnation of Andi." Or that this past weekend, we celebrated your baby sister's wedding with a huge reception, where we danced and drank and danced some more. It was a wonderful time.

Yet, in the corner of that reception room was a table of pictures honoring family members who had passed away. I saw the picture of you smiling, the flicker of a votive candle illuminating your face. Frozen in time. It has slightly faded in the two decades since you've been gone.

So much more has happened, but how do I say it all except perhaps to start from the beginning? To write this awful tale, purge it from the depths of my soul in hopes that something beautiful can come from it.

The Bible says God gives beauty for ashes. Wipes our tears away. Redeems us and gives us eternal life if we believe. Let me tell you, that has been a hard pill for me to swallow because I still hurt. Not always, not like in the beginning, but at times, that demon pokes my scarred heart; sometimes, the scab is ripped off by a song, or a smell, or by thinking I see you in a crowd. Or when I try to remember your voice. And when that happens, it takes me back to the moment I was told you were dead.

Murdered.

12-year-olds shouldn't be murdered.

Seeing the votive candlelight on your face as your sister danced with her new husband this weekend was bittersweet. Life does indeed move forward even when you feel trapped in time. Between you and your two sisters, my heart is divided into three parts. At times, it has been difficult to live life to the fullest when a third of your heart has been *stolen*.

God help me; it has been so difficult.

HAPPY BIRTHDAY KRISTIN

"My sister Andi was the best sister in the whole world. One day, she taught me a lesson. She said, *'Kristin, if you ever get into trouble, run to Pa-Pa Taylor; he will always take care of you.'* Andi loved me so much. I miss her. She died on my birthday."

Kristin Sanders, Andi's youngest sister

CHAPTER 1
SATURDAY
MAY 15, 1999
2:00 PM

It should have been a beautiful day.

A cake, four candles, balloons, and a bunch of kids running around the Play Place at McDonald's. Laughter and screams of delight, presents, smiles, and a hug from a friend. Small shoes lined up on the shelves, leaps into the ball pit, a place that brought squeals of pleasure from children and cringes from parents who knew that socks, French fries, chicken nuggets, and bits of hamburger lay beneath that sea of colored balls.

Kristin's fourth birthday party at McDonald's was a success. She was especially thrilled that her best friend Victoria was there. The two girls had attended preschool together since they were a year old. Victoria, a little girl with dark hair and shimmering blue eyes, giggled as she took my youngest daughter by the hand and pulled her toward the Play Place.

As I watched the children playing, I made a mental note to

call Andi that evening and let her wish her baby sister a "Happy Birthday." Andi, my 12-year-old daughter, had recently decided that she wanted to live with her father for a while after her new baby half-brother had been born.

After the party, my husband Kris, my middle daughter Melanie, Kristin, and I decided to go to the local rural fire department for their annual picnic. My mother, Ann, an emergency medical technician for the rural town of Collinsville, Oklahoma, had insisted it would be a great way to end the day. We didn't regret the decision. There were free hot dogs, games, and prizes. We watched Tulsa Life Flight land their helicopter, and the kids were thrilled to be able to explore the inside of the aircraft. One of the paramedics from the flight service asked if it was okay to take Kristin for a helicopter ride since it was her fourth birthday.

She looked at me with anticipation.

"Would you like to take a ride in the helicopter?"

"Yes, can I?" she asked.

"If you want to," I said.

She nodded.

The pilot scooped her up in his arms and whisked her away. The helicopter blades began to churn frantically as the chopper lifted off the ground. Kristin waved to me with her chubby baby hand. My hair whipped wildly as I watched her little face peering from the helicopter window; it grew smaller and smaller the higher it went.

The dust and debris whirled like an Oklahoma tornado. The craft hovered momentarily; she was waving and smiling when the craft shot skyward.

For a moment, panic gripped my heart. What if they crashed? I could never live with myself if anything happened to one of my children. I shook off the thought and waved back at my incredibly brave 4-year-old.

That got me thinking about all three of my daughters and how they were very similar yet so different. Andi, the eldest, was strong-willed and extroverted. Melanie was more of an introvert. I glanced around, and she was swinging on the swing set, waving up at the helicopter. Kristin was a mixture of both of her sisters and was set apart all at the same time. Genetics was a strange thing.

I watched the helicopter become a dot in the sky, and my mind wandered back 12 years to the beginning of the road of motherhood for me. I was sixteen, a kid, when I missed my period, and lo and behold, the pee stick turned blue. I was pregnant. I was much too young to be running around having unprotected sex. It was September 1986. Truth be told, I needed and craved discipline. However, the story continued with all the breathless abandon of a bad teenage problem novel.

Greg Brewer was my high school sweetheart. He had graduated from high school the previous spring, and we had plans to marry after I graduated. The baby sped things up.

After the drama of telling our parents that I was pregnant and calming everyone down from the fact that I had ruined my life and would never go to college or even graduate from high school (I had since done both).

I gave birth to a little girl at 6:06 PM on April 10, 1987. We named her Andria Nichole. One of the first things I noticed was her small nose, a tiny nub settled on the tip of her face. I inspected her body after she was born and was in awe that something so precious and wonderful had been entrusted to me. Giving birth was the most painful thing I had ever experienced, but I quickly forgot when they laid my six-pound, four-ounce daughter in my arms. For the first time, I felt like I'd done something right, and I knew the birth of this child would impact my life in a huge way. I just had no idea at the time how huge that impact would be. Andi was 20 months old when I gave birth to a second daughter, Melanie. Turns out, the two girls were the only good thing that came out of that shotgun marriage. We divorced after four years of marriage.

After the divorce, I left Arkansas with the girls, and life was pretty good for the three of us. We moved to Collinsville, Oklahoma, a suburb of Tulsa. I began working as an emergency medical technician and enrolled in paramedic school.

Several years later, I remarried a firefighter named Kris DeMauro. We met in July of 1992. He was teaching an emergency medical technician refresher course at the vocational school I was attending. I was late for class. I tried to slip into the room unnoticed. He called me out and asked my name in front of everyone. With all eyes on me, I muttered "Rebecca" and slid into my chair. I wanted to crawl under the table. He didn't know that I had barely made it to the course because my old Monte Carlo was on its last leg. I limped it into the school parking lot after leaving a trail of heavy black smoke all the way down Memorial Drive.

We began dating and finally married on a snowy day in March 1994. We drove to Rogers, Arkansas, and walked out onto a bluff overlooking Beaver Lake, a place where I practically grew up. The ceremony was beautiful. We said our vows in a foot of snow, and birds chattered in the background.

On May 15, 1995, Kris and I had a child of our own. We named her Kristin Elizabeth. With my two girls, Andi and Melanie, and his son, Kristofer, from his first marriage, we became a blended family. Our family had many good times together. We built campfires in our backyard, roasted hotdogs and marshmallows, and ate until we were stuffed. We had a small plastic pool in the backyard that was about two feet deep for the kids to swim in. One day, I looked out the back window, and Kris was in the pool with the kids. Being 6'3", he took up most of the pool, but the kids didn't seem to mind. They were jumping and splashing and having a great time. They rode on his back like he was a majestic sea monster, and the smiles and laughter were plentiful. I snapped some pictures of those golden moments. Then I brought them some homemade grape Popsicles that we had made from Kool-Aid. Kris ate one right along with the kids as they sat on the lawn to dry off. Our Cocker Spaniel, Lady, jumped around, licking Popsicle juice off their arms. It was a picturesque moment. We had many memories like those.

The trouble began when Andi was ten and a half and decided she wanted to live with her dad and his new wife, who had just given birth to a baby boy. It was extremely difficult because we had wanted Andi to stay with us. My heart broke at the thought of her desire to move away from us, from me. I felt that I had failed in some way as a mother. At first, I said she couldn't go, but Andi persisted.

"I just want to move to Arkansas so I can spend time with

my new baby brother."

I felt betrayed. I was angry. After a few months in a very uproarious household, I sat down with Kris and told him I thought we should let Andi try living with her dad for a while, just to see how it would work out. He said he thought it was a bad idea; she needed to be with us. He told me he had a bad feeling about it. I retorted that he was overreacting. We needed peace in our home.

It was then that I made the worst decision I had ever made in my life. I informed Kris that I was letting Andi go, reassuring him that she would be back in a few months, putting an end to this entire mess.

In October of 1997, Andi's dad, wife, and new brother came to our Oklahoma home to pick Andi up. When they arrived, I wanted to grab my daughter around the waist and force her back into the house. As they loaded all her belongings into the car, I just knew she would change her mind, especially when she hugged me and began to weep in my arms. At that moment, I was sure she would stay. She belonged here with us, not with them.

"I'll miss you so bad, Mommy."

My voice cracked, and I told Andi we would be together every other weekend during school breaks and summer vacation. I promised to call her every Sunday. I attempted to smile despite my deep sadness. She opened the car door, sat down in the backseat, and clicked her seat belt. Tears streaked down her little round face. The slamming of the car door screamed finality. She looked into my eyes and mouthed the words, "I love you."

"I love you back," I said.

I knew in my heart she felt pulled between her father and me—she always had. She never wanted us to divorce. She wanted us to get back together and was quite vocal about it, saying things like, "When you and Daddy get back together, it will be so nice. We can do things as a family again."

The sad thing was that we were never much of a family in the first place. I tried to explain to Andi that Greg and I were never going to get back together, but she blocked that from her mind. She loved us both and wanted us together. She was very loyal to us both.

When the car backed out of the driveway, I felt sick to my stomach. As they drove away, I expected to see the taillights light up as they turned around to bring her back, but the car disappeared out of sight.

Up until then, my life had consisted of catering to my children. Now, my oldest child was gone. It was as though a part of me was missing; a part of my heart died when she left. I could never shake the feeling that it was wrong to let her go. I was so torn between making her happy and making her live with me. There was no parenting manual on what to do in a situation like this, so I did what I thought was right. I let her go.

I soon discovered Andi loved living in the country. Her dad

taught her to hunt and fish. She rode her four-wheeler in the woods, played basketball for the Hatfield Bobcats in the small community south of Mena, and was very content. I had begun to accept that things were okay.

I was wrong.

Just over a year of her living in Arkansas, May 15, 1999, rolled around. The day that had started so wonderfully turned out to be the day that would wreck our lives.

CHAPTER 2
MISSING
SATURDAY
MAY 15, 1999
7:30 PM

Andi glanced out the window toward her grandparents' house. She could not see it through the line of trees, but it was close by, and she knew it was there. She wished she were over there, spending time with Grandpa and Grandma instead of being stuck at her father and stepmother's home, where she was starting to feel trapped.

That was what the fight had been about. That was why she was stuck there today. The night before, she had quarreled with her dad and his wife about the fact that she always wanted to be at her grandparents', never there. The fight had gotten so ugly that she was now grounded for the weekend to that house—where she had so many responsibilities: cooking, cleaning, and babysitting.

Only two weeks more and school would be out. Only two weeks more and she could go to Mommy and Kris's house for the summer, and secretly, she hoped, for good. She had confided this to her sister, Melanie, by phone. She had made Melanie promise not to tell. She didn't want to cause any trouble. But she couldn't help it. She was starting to hate it there.

Greg came into the doorway. Stepmother was at work. Andi was still smarting over the things that had been said the night before, though she had already forgiven her father. Forgiving him had always been easy for her for some reason.

"I'm going down to the pond to fish," he said.

She wished he would say, "Do you want to come with me?" But instead, he said, "I need you to watch the kids."

"Okay," she mumbled, giving no argument.

Only two weeks more...

He had been quietly stalking. Trolling her. Peeking in her window. He had even caught a glimpse up her dress once at a family function.

Following without her knowing. Without anyone knowing.

The fantasies had grown dark, thinking of the things he could do to her. He had been watching her for months.

She didn't know it. No one did.

Andi waved out the door as her father headed down the road toward the pond. She sighed wistfully and then turned as one of her stepsiblings tugged on her shirttail, needing something. She was wearing a tee shirt that read, "Heaven's Gates, Hell's Flames...Is your name in the book?" Mommy had bought her that shirt when they had attended the Heaven's Gates, Hell's Flames event in Tulsa, which was a drama set up in a spook-house type format, depicting the gates of heaven or horrors of hell.

She needed some new clothes. Maybe when she got back home with Mommy, they could go shopping. She loved to shop with Mommy.

It was dinner time, and once again, he was forced to visit his in-laws. He hated them, especially his mother-in-law, but his wife was already there, and he could not stand to have her out of his sight for long. On the way, he passed the house where Andi lived. Greg's truck was gone. But Andi was there, he was sure of it. He would play his drums first. He always felt better when he played his drums, and he could be there to supervise his wife without having to talk to her parents. He dragged the drum set outside, cranked up the hard rock station on the radio, and started to play, pounding all his anger and frustration onto the drum set, making short work of a six-pack of Miller beer, keeping an ever-watchful eye on his wife's comings and goings. Wife called that dinner was ready. Salmon patties and taters. Iced tea. When he finished eating, he could return to the drums. He looked toward Greg's house instead.

There was someone knocking at the door.

Andi adjusted the heat on the Fry Daddy cooker. The chicken she had just dropped into the grease crackled inside, but she knew it would be a moment before it was ready to take out. She would be right back. It should be fine.

A man was at the door. Andi knew the man, or she wouldn't have opened it. He spoke to her, startling her with his words, words that made her forget her siblings in the living room, the chicken in the fryer, no shoes on her feet. Her siblings stared at the open door, waiting for her return. She didn't come back.

Where did Andi go?

SATURDAY
MAY 15, 1999
9:00 PM

The phone rang. Andi's call, I was sure of it. The perfect ending to a perfect day.

Andi's voice was not on the other end. It was Greg's sister, Trina. She didn't greet me; she said, "Andi's missing."

Words. Words that at first shocked me as if I had been slapped across the cheek. Then, the slow, stinging sensation spread across my skin, turning to a burn, letting me know I had truly been struck.

I held the phone to my ear for a moment, trying to absorb

what she was telling me.

"The police are here," Trina continued. Short puffs of breath. Slap. Slap. Slap again. "We think she left with some of her friends. She has run off somewhere. Don't worry."

Don't worry?

I looked out the window. Dusk was blanketing the land, heralding the darkness of night. Andi was afraid of the dark. She would never stay out in the pitch-blackness of night.

"Where is she?" My question was automatic.

Trina repeated, "We don't know, but the police will find her. I am sure of it. Don't panic; everything will be okay."

She was scared. I knew it. I hung up the phone, in disbelief, looked at Kris, and struck him as I had been struck. "Andi's missing."

The same delayed reaction. The same question. "What, where is she?"

"They don't know. The police are looking."

"The police? Oh, God."

We stared at each other for a few seconds. Then I ran to the bedroom and began throwing clothes into a suitcase.

I felt sick. Sick. Don't throw up, don't throw up, oh my God. She wouldn't run off without telling anyone where she was going; she had always been so responsible. Don't throw up, stop shaking.

Stop shaking!

Kris's voice broke into my wild, rambling thoughts. "Where are you going?"

Standing in the doorway, he looked as helpless as I felt, and a wave of irrational irritation surged through me.

"To Arkansas, to look for her. Where else do you think I would be going?"

"Rebecca, calm down," he said. "It's going to be okay."

I kept throwing clothes into the suitcase. Panic clutched my lungs, paralyzing them so that my breath came in quick, ineffective puffs. I would not calm down. Andi was terrified. I knew it.

And I had told her she was a scaredy cat. I remembered it suddenly at that moment. A few weeks prior, when she had been visiting on spring break, she had come into my bedroom at bedtime.

"Mommy, I'm scared to sleep in the other room by myself. Can I sleep in here with you?"

"Don't be a big scaredy cat," I had said. "You'll be fine. Go to bed. I'm literally twenty feet away. I can see your door from here. I'll make pancakes in the morning, chocolate chip." I smiled. She lowered her shoulders and slumped away.

Thinking back, I felt so guilty about saying those words to her. I had called my daughter a scaredy cat. What kind of mother was I? How could I have done that?

Kris and I loaded up and headed to my mother and stepdad's house. Taking charge of a situation that was quickly spinning out of control, he informed me that he and my stepdad, Lloyd Allen, would go to Hatfield to assist in the search. Kris assured me they would bring her home, and I wanted to believe him. But I had a bad feeling.

A very bad feeling.

Meanwhile, in Mena, search parties had formed and were scouring the county for any sign of Andi. They searched the hangouts, thick forests, abandoned buildings, and cars. They checked with all her young friends from school, but no one had a clue where Andi had gone.

Nobody, that is, except her younger step-siblings, Samantha and Torrey, ages 8 and 6, whom Andi had been babysitting. They were very direct from the beginning.

"Uncle Karl took her away in his red truck. He knocked on the door and told her she had to come with him," Samantha said. "He said something was wrong with Grandma and Grandpa Brewer. She told us she would be right back."

Uncle Karl? Greg's brother-in-law, her paternal aunt Trina's husband? What would he have to do with any of this?

Aunt Trina disputed this. She kept telling the children not to say anything like that to the police because it could get Karl in trouble. Besides, Karl had left the elder Brewers' residence at 7:30

to visit his parents in Cove, which was ten miles to the south. It was concluded that Andi had left with someone with dark hair, like Karl, and in a red truck. Another factor in the dispute was that the two young eyewitnesses both had extremely poor eyesight and were not wearing their glasses. These were all questions weighing heavily upon the police. The fact that Andi had gotten into a dispute with Greg and his wife the night before led them to believe she was a possible runaway. Law enforcement didn't know our daughter well enough to realize that I knew she wouldn't run away. They were going on their past experiences with runaways. I knew Andi was afraid of her own shadow. I also knew that she would never leave her younger stepsiblings alone. There were too many unanswered questions to simply assume that she could have taken off without telling anyone. When she left, she told the children she would be right back. If she were going to run away, she would have taken more than the clothes on her back, would have been wearing shoes, and wouldn't have left chicken frying in the Fry Daddy cooker.

I knew the area well, having grown up in Hatfield. It would have been possible for someone to drive up the dirt drive where Greg's triple-wide trailer was located, snatch Andi, and drive away without being seen, even though her grandparents' home was a mere four hundred yards away; thick, dense woods separated the two homes. I knew deep down that Andi did not run away. Deep inside of me, I knew something was wrong, bad wrong. Something told me she had been taken. **Stolen.**

SATURDAY
MAY 15, 1999
10:00 PM

My sister, Kristy, wrung her hands. I drummed my fingers on the kitchen table. Mom flitted aimlessly around the kitchen, from one task to another. The conversation came and went, hitting the shore with the same predictable wave.

Where could she be? I didn't know. Should we go to Arkansas now? Wait and see what they found out.

The phone rang. Mom answered and then handed me the phone.

"Becc, this is Sheriff Oglesby."

So official. I knew him as Mike, my stepdad's old buddy from high school.

"Here's what we have up to this point. Trina (Brewer) Roberts called our 911 Center at about 8:40 PM and reported Andi missing. I sent a deputy to Charles and Ann Brewer's house to take a report. Then I went ahead and went over myself. The kids informed them she had left with a man in a red truck. Andi told the children she would be right back. I found out she had a disagreement with Greg and Carla last night. We think she has taken off with some friends. We are in the process of interviewing all her friends and looking for the red truck. Just want you to know."

"Don't worry about any of this. We see kids get mad and

take off all the time. We will find her and bring her back."

If one more person told me not to worry again, I would slap them.

"I just can't see her running away, Sheriff. You don't know her. She isn't like that. She's too scared. You don't know her."

Don't be such a scaredy cat...oh my god, Andi, I'm so sorry.

"It's going to be okay, trust me. This will all be over by morning. I have to get to work; I will keep in touch."

"Thank you." I hung up the phone. Mom and Kristy were staring at me.

"What did he say?" Kristy asked.

"He assured me that kids run off all the time and they would find her."

"Good," Mom said.

"I am still scared, though."

Mom turned away quickly and scrubbed the counter briskly. Kristy took my hand and looked into my eyes. "Me, too."

Where could she be? I didn't know.

Should we go to Arkansas now?

Wait and see...

SUNDAY
MAY 16, 1999
12:30 AM

I called my dad in Lawrence, Kansas. He would be on his way soon. Maybe he could fix this.

I sat on Mom's couch and stared at the wall clock. Tick, tock, tick, tock. Chime. Another hour. The clock was my enemy, and I faced time alone. Melanie and Kristin were sleeping in the guest room. Mom had decided to stop trying to scrub the dirt off the earth and lie down as well. I knew she wasn't asleep. She should have stayed up with me, kept me company, our voices drowning out the silence, the clock, my thoughts. Instead, I was alone, tortured in a state of not knowing.

The not knowing was killing me.

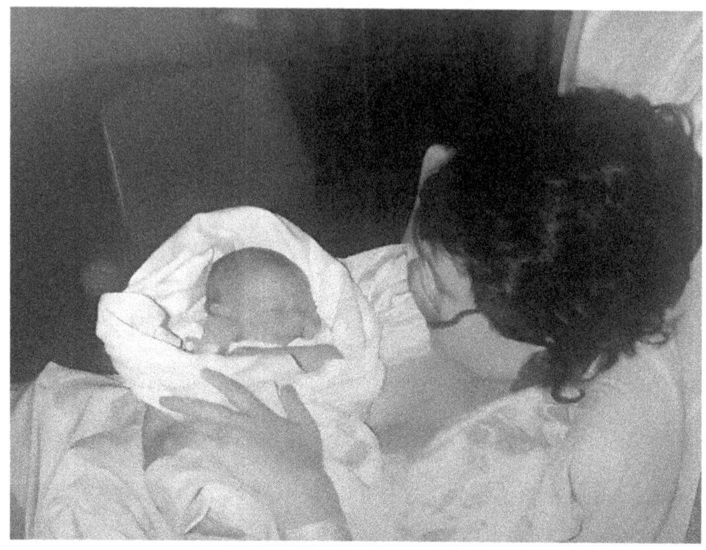

Baby girl, your hair was dark blonde when you were born, golden brown later. Your eyes are golden brown, too, flecked with green. When you smile, those eyes make little slits on your face like Kristy's. But it is your lips that mark you as a Petty—pouty and full, like mine and my sister's, like my father's, like his father's. And yet, you are Brewer, too, tall like your grandmother Ann. A mix of all of us. How could you not capture all our hearts? You are us.

We belong to you, as well. You always want to be the center of attention, the only one on the stage. You command the room. You want the audience to love you. And we do.

I saw my stepdad's big rubber boots by the front door caked in mud and thought about you when you were three years old, following Grandpa Taylor around feeding his chickens on the farm. You in your high rubber boots, looking like a miniature version of him, tossing feed to the birds and giggling in that high-pitched way you did. Then, seeing Memaw Taylor on the porch hollering for you and Papa to come and eat, smiling from ear to ear as she watched you two hand in hand. I thought about all the time they had spent helping me raise you, their first grandchild. Babysitting while I worked long hours to help put food on the table, long hours that I wished I could take back and spend in a better way.

Then I thought about coming to their house to pick you and

Melanie up in the evening, how you would want to stay with them because they spoiled you rotten, which was okay. Grandparents were supposed to do that, right? I could still see your little legs scissoring toward my mother and running into her arms with me chasing close behind after I pronounced it was time to go home.

But I couldn't chase you now. I wouldn't know where to run. Was this a practical joke? Because if it was, this wasn't funny. No. You wouldn't play a joke like this, you wouldn't run away, you wouldn't make us all worry on purpose. You were us. Please call and let us know if you are okay. Please send a message, somehow, some way. I had to know you were okay. I could never sleep again until I knew you were safe.

This was torture. The worst kind of torture.

SUNDAY
MAY 16, 1999
6:00 AM

The phone rang. I rose stiffly from my night-long station on the couch, my neck aching. I hoped it was Kris... but only if he was going to tell me what I wanted to hear. My heart leaped at the sound of his voice but then fell at his tone. He sounded tired, and his words did nothing to ease my apprehension.

"It's like she's vanished into thin air. We've looked everywhere. All through the woods, every abandoned building.

We've talked to all her friends. The police are searching for all red trucks. Search parties are looking all over the county."

He paused, probably waiting for an answer from me. I had nothing to give.

"This is getting scary, Becc."

When had it ever stopped being scary? I started to cry. "I'm coming down there. Mom and I will be there in a few hours."

A part of me wished he would say, "No need, it's going to be okay, we'll find her soon." It wouldn't stop me from coming, but it would make me feel better. But he just said, "Sheriff Oglesby told us that if she is not found by 10:30 this morning, they are turning her disappearance into a criminal investigation."

"Are you saying they believe she was kidnapped?"

"They said they are leaning toward that but are still hopeful that she may be hiding in the woods with a boy."

"That's ludicrous. She wouldn't do that." Even as I said it, I prayed she had done exactly that. I could handle anything if she were okay.

"That's just what they told me," he replied.

I sat down. I had no choice; my knees were very weak.

SUNDAY
MAY 16, 1999
7:30 AM

Mom and I knew it was time to go to Hatfield. On our way, an awkward silence fell inside the truck. After many miles, I broke the silence and said, "I should never have let her move. This is all my fault."

I wanted my mother to reassure me otherwise. But she just said, "Let's not think about that now."

I shouldn't have expected anything diffcrent; in fact, I was glad she didn't say, "I told you so." Mom and Lloyd Allen had been adamant in their objections to Andi's moving. They had even suggested she come live with them instead, but they never understood that Andi's desire to go to Arkansas had nothing to do with escaping from me... she just wanted to be with her father.

"What if she's not okay? I have a really bad feeling, Mom."

Her silence told me she did, too.

"I am so scared." I took a deep breath and set my jaw in determination. "When they find her, she is moving back to Tulsa with us. Letting her move was the stupidest thing I have ever done.

" "Yes, it was," she snapped.

I felt awful.

Then, she took a deep breath and said more gently, "Let's

not think the worst. Let's just go to Mena and find out what's going on."

"Okay," I said. I spent the rest of the trip to Mena silently begging God for my daughter's safe return.

We arrived in Polk County. Mena, Arkansas, a town of approximately 5,000 people, was the county seat and was built for the Kansas City Pittsburg and Gulf Railroad (KCP&G). The railroad was later called the Kansas City Southern. The KCP&G established Mena as the dividing point along the line from Kansas City to Port Arthur, Texas. It ensured the establishment of the town, and by the time the railroad moved the dividing point to Heavener, Oklahoma, it was able to stand on its own.

The railroad left its mark on the town, and the Mena Depot still stood today. Trains blared through town, but most folks didn't even hear them anymore after growing accustomed to the whistle and roar of the steam engines.

Tourism was a big moneymaker in Mena with 82,000 visitors a year, most coming to visit Queen Wilhelmina State Park located atop beautiful Rich Mountain. Each year, the fall foliage attracts many to come and gaze at the wonder and beauty of the changing colors. The 54-mile scenic drive from Mena, Arkansas, to Talihina, Oklahoma, was famous throughout the United States.

Like those thousands of tourists who trekked through every

year, I normally enjoyed this trip, looked forward to it even. But on this day, beautiful Rich Mountain or Queen Wilhelmina State Park looked ugly to me. As my eyes panned the mountainous range, I realized this picturesque scene was a wilderness, one in which my child was possibly lost. My breath caught in my throat as I realized the magnitude of the search area, the valleys and hills and brambles and creeks and caves and rocks and snakes and ticks and dirt and branch-littered paths that would have to be combed to find anyone who was lost there—much less a five-foot, 110-pound girl.

The wilderness terrified me, but something else surmounted even that. At the first stoplight in town, we noticed the unmarked vehicle in front of us. Several radio antennas poked from its roof, and the tag read "U.S. Government." Having been a paramedic in the past, I knew this to be an FBI vehicle. I didn't point this out to my mother. The vehicle turned right and headed toward the police department. I watched it disappear, my heart exploding in my chest. Sweat trickled down my back, and I caught a vision of my ashen face and the worry-etched brow in the rearview mirror.

The FBI didn't come to town for a runaway.

SUNDAY
MAY 16, 1999
10:30 AM

We arrived at what law enforcement was now calling "The Command Post": Greg's parents' home. The Brewers' yard looked like an anthill swarming with people: neighbors, relatives, friends, law enforcement, and news media. I stared at the sea of people before me. Panic and anger rose in me, too. It was a scary situation, but I hadn't realized how serious the investigation had become. Why hadn't I been told more? Why had everyone tried to sugarcoat the truth?

I got out of the truck and weaved my way through the masses. I approached the porch and recognized the man sitting in the chair beside the front door. He seemed oddly out of place, as everyone was milling and talking in near panic mode, and he simply sat there, whittling, whittling, whittling, his hands working in a frantic motion.

Karl Roberts.

Uncle Karl.

He made no eye contact with anyone until I opened the gate and walked onto the covered porch area. He looked up at me as I passed, and I said, "How are you, Karl?"

"Fine. The police want to talk to me about Andi," he blurted.

I stopped and listened as he rambled on, "They say that since

I fit the description, they need to interview me. You know, they can hook me up to a lie detector and search my truck if they want. I didn't have anything to do with this; I have nothing to hide."

I sighed. I really didn't have time to make Karl Roberts feel better when I was worried about my daughter.

"Well, Karl, if you don't have anything to do with this, then you have nothing to worry about. I would just chill if I were you. They will sort it out."

"I think Bobby Stone has something to do with it," he said, going back to his whittling. "He drives a red truck and fits the description."

Bobby Stone was a family friend of the Brewers who had recently graduated from Hatfield High School.

"Do you think Andi ran away with Bobby Stone?" I asked.

Bobby was eighteen. Surely, he wouldn't want to run away with a 12-year-old little girl.

Karl didn't look up from his whittling again. I excused myself and walked into the house, where Greg's mother, Ann, embraced me, holding onto me for what seemed like forever.

"I'm so scared, Becki. What if she's lying out there somewhere hurt, and we can't find her?" she asked, almost sobbing.

"We will find her," I said, wishing I could believe my own words.

My years in Arkansas and Oklahoma had taught me something about Southerners: if there was a crisis, there would be food. No one might feel like eating it, but everyone would bring their best casserole, cobbler, or cake to the troubled family's home. So, I was not surprised to see the Brewers' table loaded down with every dish imaginable. Someone offered to fix me a plate, but I couldn't even think about eating. All I could do was glance time after time out the window, hoping a police car would pull into the driveway with Andi in the backseat.

I envisioned the moment. Her tear-stained face filled with relief at being home. I would rush out to meet her, filled with joy and yet mad as hell that she had scared me and everyone else half to death. All would be forgiven, though, because I would just be happy she was safe. I needed that moment I was envisioning. I needed my daughter to come back.

At that point, I had already forgotten my strange conversation with Uncle Karl, and it seemed unimportant. Later, he joined one of the search parties and combed the woods to find his missing niece. He seemed to be genuinely concerned for her well-being and safe return.

Andi's paternal grandfather, Pa, Charles Brewer, later recounted that after the search, he sat down at the kitchen table with Karl and discussed what he would do to a person if they ever kidnapped or harmed one of his two young children.

"I will kill someone if they hurt my babies," Karl said.

"I'll kill someone if they have hurt my baby, Andi," Pa said.

Shortly afterward, Pa saw Karl walk out to the front of his pickup and pull out some twigs that were stuck in the front bumper. This struck him as odd, knowing that Karl was not a hunter; therefore, his truck never left the paved road. He wondered why and how Karl got twigs stuck in his front bumper. He began to realize that perhaps, just perhaps, Karl knew where Andi was located.

Pa was right.

CHAPTER 3
THE DEVIL IN POLK COUNTY

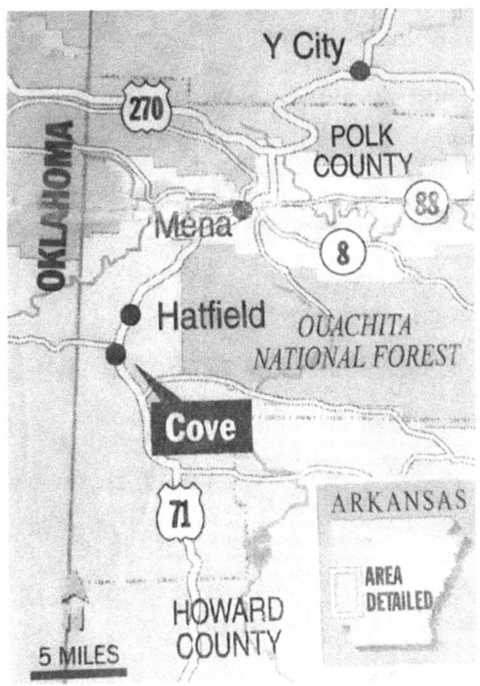

Polk County was formed in 1844 from part of Sevier County and was named for U.S. President James K. Polk. The county seat was Mena. Long, narrow ridges of folded rock, large fertile valleys, and mountains covered with oak and pine trees made up the landscape of the county. Nearly half of Polk County lay in the Ouachita National Forest.

Karl Douglas Roberts was no stranger to me. He had graduated from high school a year ahead of me in a neighboring town. He dated a girl named Lori off and on at the high school I attended, which was how I became acquainted with him. I remember very vividly that he would drive around the school every day at lunch to check on Lori. He was very controlling of her, afraid another boy might talk to her. The high school kids would stand around the picnic tables outside during lunch at Hatfield High School, talking and laughing, having a good time. Then, in the distance, we could hear the 'BOOM, BOOM, BOOM' of his truck stereo, blaring hard rock music. He would drive back and forth, holding his arm out the window, giving us the devil sign, which was a closed fist with the pointer and pinky finger extended, and sticking out his tongue like Gene Simmons from KISS. When he drove by, a hush would fall on all the students. Many of us were genuinely scared. He had an evil feel that seemed to permeate from him. We all nicknamed him "devil." Not because of the loud music or the devil sign he would give, but because he told everyone he worshiped Satan. He held seances, told us he had given his soul to Lucifer, and played the part very well.

My sister, Kristy, saw him one night at McLain's drive-in, a local hangout where all the teenagers went to play pool and eat cheeseburgers. That night, he was parked around the back of the restaurant. Karl was standing outside his truck listening to Motley Crue's song "Shout at the Devil." He told my sister he was turning into Satan himself and asked her to feel the horns growing on top of his head. A bit nervous, Kristy stood up to him and said, "Karl, you're not the devil and don't have horns on your head."

"Yes, I do, feel them," he said, running his fingers through his dark curly hair, blue eyes flashing wildly.

Kristy rolled her eyes.

Even though I firmly believed he just did it to get attention, his girlfriend, Lori, was a believer. She told stories of how his eyes would change colors when he was mad and how he controlled her every move. She told of the demonic chants he would recite around local campfires or in the graveyard. She swore that when he became angry, his voice would change. He smoked pot and drank county-line beer and gave glory to his savior... Satan. He also claimed he took a blood covenant with him and was eager to tell anyone and everyone about it. He wore an upside-down crucifix around his neck that had a switchblade hidden inside; he would often pull it out to scare others. It was even rumored that he attended a local church service where they had tried to perform an exorcism to "cast" the devil out of him. They said he writhed around on the floor and foamed at the mouth, but I just figured he'd seen the movie *The Exorcist* and was just putting on a good show.

It was not until four years later that Karl Douglas Roberts

became a part of my life again. He began to date Greg's sister, Trina. When she told me that she had met someone, I eagerly wanted to know who because she had not dated anyone seriously.

When she told me, I was stunned, "You're dating Devil?"

She assured me that Karl didn't worship Satan and was a nice guy. She said the Satan worship was an act for attention.

It was no surprise when she decided to marry him about a year later. She asked me to be the matron of honor. I agreed. Everyone was awestruck at the change Trina had seemed to have made in Karl. He was no longer a rebellious teenager who dabbled in Satanism but a young man content and happy, grown-up even. He was in love and ready to settle down with his young bride.

I walked down the aisle on the arm of Karl's brother, Robert. The church was packed. Karl's face lit up when his bride stepped into the room. They seemed very happy. I silently scolded myself for scoffing at her groom when I was in school. He was just a kid who needed to be loved. Now, he had a new wife, and they were starting a life together.

I saw two-year-old Andria and baby Melanie with their father, Greg, in the crowd. They were wearing pretty little dresses, their hair donned with bows and barrettes. They looked darling. Two little angels.

Karl and Trina moved into a small mobile home in nearby Cove, Arkansas. He got a job building bridges for a local contracting company. She worked for a grocery store in town. But soon, Karl's jealousy reappeared. Trina wasn't allowed to have friends, and he kept track of the mileage on her vehicle, often accusing her of cheating on him.

Later in the marriage, he would become so enraged and overcome with jealousy that he would visualize seeing her with other men. He thought he would see her driving around town, sitting next to her lover. In fact, Trina was completely faithful and never considered cheating on him. At times, he would become so enraged with her that he became physically violent, often choking her out. When she woke up, he apologized, begging her not to leave. She always forgave him and stayed. She never told a soul that he was violent.

They frequented the house of her parents, Charles and Ann Brewer. Karl was very jealous of Trina's relationship with her mother. However, she refused to let him come between her and her family. Since I was part of the family at the time, she was allowed to be my friend... for a while.

Then, one day, he sent Trina and me to the beer joint across the county line (Polk County was a dry county) to get him some beer. He liked to drink beer and play his drums, which he was very proficient at; in fact, he was one of the best drummers I had ever heard. He was self-taught.

When we returned, he snapped, "What took you so long?"

Trina seemed nervous to answer, and to lighten the mood, I piped, in my typical joking fashion, "Aw, we were flirting with a couple of cute guys." Which wasn't true at all.

I didn't know she got in a lot of trouble for my comment. Later, she was choked to the point of passing out because of a comment I had made in a joking manner. After that, Trina was no longer allowed to go anywhere with me, and Karl would sneer and roll his eyes at me when I came around her. I was confused that my sister-in-law was no longer allowed to barely talk to me.

Finally, Karl and Trina came to an agreement concerning Trina's family, particularly her mother and me. He set up his drum set at her parents' house and played music in an outbuilding while she visited her family. They made these visits most days.

Greg, the girls, and I lived at the same address from which Andi would later disappear, 400 yards up a shrouded driveway from his parents' home. Because of the thick foliage, we couldn't see his parents' house, but we could tell when Karl and Trina were visiting by the sound of Karl's pounding drums. He would turn on heavy metal music and play right along with Motley Crue, ACDC, and any heavy metal band he took a liking to. He was in tip-top shape, solid as a rock, from the bridgework and playing his drums. He hardly ever spoke to me any longer, and he never talked to the girls. He stayed away from us as much as possible. At the time, I was in the dark about his abusive behavior toward Trina and had no clue of the evil brewing back inside him.

Karl and Trina married in 1989, and I divorced Greg and moved to Tulsa with the girls in 1992. Karl Roberts was officially my brother-in-law for three years, but he would be a part of my life forever.

CHAPTER 4
STILL MISSING
SUNDAY
MAY 16, 1999

FBI Official Transcript:

On the evening of May 16, 1999, Friend of Andria Brewer, learning of her disappearance, Friend stated she had a dream wherein Friend was at a church in Cove, Arkansas, and observed Andria Brewer. Brewer, in the dream, told Friend that she had to leave and that she couldn't stay. Friend then saw Brewer running toward a mountain or a hill near the church in a field. Brewer ran through an opening in a barbed-wire fence. Friend further described the field as having a number of large stumps pushed together with briars in the corner. Behind the field was a dirt road. Friend recalled that in her dream, she rode a four-wheeler on this road and heard Brewer screaming for help.

11-year-old Friend of Andria Brewer (Name Omitted)

SUNDAY
MAY 16, 1999
1:30 PM

Everyone wanted to talk to me and Greg. Cameras were rolling, microphones shoved near our faces. And I was begging. Me. Rebecca, who never begged anyone for anything. Me, who drove two little girls to Tulsa to start my life over after a tumultuous marriage, worked two jobs, and went to paramedic school. Me. Rebecca. Sitting there in front of a television camera, sobbing like a baby, begging some stranger for my child's life. I felt so heartbroken. I did not care.

"Please bring her back, please, we love her and miss her so much. She means the world to us; we just want her to come home. Andi, if you are out there watching us, I'm begging you to call us. We will come to get you. Please call us."

Please.

"Is there anything else you would add if you could speak to Andi right now?"

I looked at Greg, expecting him to say something. Anything. And he didn't look up at the camera. He sat with his head down, hands firmly clasped together. And he was silent. He could not speak. His bottom lip was quivering. Why couldn't he speak? I wondered why he even sat down next to me in the lawn chair the cameraman had pulled up for him. I wanted to shake him. Say something. Anything. I felt so alone, even with him beside me. It was all on me, and I could do nothing except cry. I briefly wondered how life could be normal one second and out of control the next.

Finally, I answered and told the reporter that no matter what had happened, we could get through it as a family. We were a family, and everything would be okay. I told her that we were not complete without her, and I addressed whoever may have taken her. I told that person that no questions would be asked; just drop her off where she could get to a phone and call us.

The interview ended without Greg ever looking up. I wiped my face with a wet washcloth someone handed me, and I happened to notice that Uncle Karl had been watching the interview from the Brewers' porch. His year-old son was perched on his hip, and Melanie was standing next to him. He turned away when I looked at him.

SUNDAY
MAY 16, 1999
3:00 PM

Search parties, police, FBI, firefighters, the media—they were everywhere. The firehouse had been turned into a command center, and we stopped by to see if there was anything we could do. I felt the need to help in some way, but I didn't know how. Some of my family members were out with the search parties; some had formed their own search parties. There was no rhyme or structure to them. Just groups of people looking in places that, had they found her, I knew she wouldn't be alive. There was no way in hell I was going out with one of the many scattered searches. Those groups weren't looking for a living child; they were looking in places for a body. No, thank you. I knew she was coming back home. I wanted no part of that.

Oh God, where is she?

SUNDAY
MAY 16,1999
8:00 PM

That evening, I felt as though I was in a revolving door, emotions swirling me around and around, into one room and out of another. Andi must be safe. So why hadn't we heard from her?

I thought about the chicken frying in the Fry-Daddy. No shoes on her feet. Now, it was getting dark for the second night of her being gone. She was sweet to take care of her stepsiblings. She cooked for them and babysat them while her dad fished in the pond nearby. My stomach dropped at the thought that she never got to eat that meal. Could it have been her last meal that she didn't get to eat? Was she hungry? Was she cold without her shoes?

Storms were rolling in tonight, the weatherman said, but his storm predictions were the second story on the news. Andi was the first. I wanted to throw up.

Was someone hurting her? Was she lying somewhere, hurt and alone? Was she calling for help? Was she calling for her dad? Was she calling for me? Could she call out at all? God, if you would just let my child come home, I promise to serve you my whole life. I've been trying so hard to be good, can't you see that? Haven't I been taking my kids to church? Trying to be a good mother? Haven't I been singing in the choir at church?

Where were you when she disappeared, anyway? No, I shouldn't think things like that. But... where were you? Where were all those angels I've been taught about? They are protecting her right now, right? You have your hand on her, don't you? I must believe that. I just must.

But where are you?

SUNDAY
MAY 16, 1999
9:00 PM

The FBI summoned us for an interview.

I was exhausted, on autopilot. We dragged ourselves into the car, out of the car, up the stairs, and into the lobby of the Mena, Arkansas police department. The tired faces of others also summoned and greeted us, including Greg's parents, Nan and Pa, and Karl Roberts. And the young man, Bobby Stone, the family friend. He was there with his father, David, and looked a trifle too nervous for me. I watched him fidget with narrowed and suspicious eyes; did he know where she was?

The FBI called him in. I heard his father say, "My son didn't have anything to do with this. He is expected to leave a week from Monday for the Marine Corps. Is this going to detain him?"

Detain him? Who the hell cared if it detained him? Who the hell cared if he was going to the Marine Corps? Where the hell was my daughter?

An FBI agent with a flat-top crew haircut approached me.

"Ma'am, can you step in here with me, please?"

I followed the FBI agent into a small room. "Hello, my name is Special Agent Falls. I'm with the FBI from Hot Springs. I will need to ask you a few questions this evening."

His voice was very official yet very soft and soothed me. A sense of peace suddenly enveloped me, as if a band of angels had descended right from the throne room of God and now surrounded me.

The FBI was on the case now. They would fix everything and fast. Andi would return soon, and when she did, we would take her right back home to Oklahoma with us. No more living with Greg and his wife. And when we got there, we would sit around the dinner table and have her favorite meal. Then we could watch her favorite movie, *Armageddon,* fifty times if she wants. She could have anything she wanted, so she would never want to leave us again.

The Flat Top Angel was asking me questions. What kind of person was Andi? Had she run away before? Had she ever gotten in trouble at school? An angel from God should already know the answers to these and the million other questions he asked, but I knew God worked in mysterious ways, so I answered them one and all.

Flat Top Angel inscribed all my answers into his heavenly book and released me back out into the world. As I left, I heard FBI agents yelling at Bobby Stone in the next room; I stopped and listened as he pleaded for them to believe him. "I didn't do it! I swear!"

Suddenly, I realized that I hoped she did run away with Bobby Stone. I hoped he did have her and that she was hidden somewhere in the woods waiting for him because that would mean she was still alive.

I passed Karl Roberts right outside the door. He pulled on his cigarette and blew smoke out into the night air. He didn't look at me this time.

**SUNDAY
MAY 16, 1999
11:30 PM**

It was almost midnight. Twenty-six hours had passed. No food. No sleep. No Andi.

It had been a week ago that I last talked to her. Mother's Day. We had talked about summer break and discussed arrangements for her summer-long visit. I heard her voice in my head.

"I sent you a Mother's Day card; Pa mailed it Monday. It's a little late, but you will like it," she said.

Better late than never.

On Wednesday, I checked my mailbox and found the card.

Mom is another word for love...I Mom You...Happy Mother's Day... Love, Andi

The thunderstorm churned outside. Lightning illuminated the edges of the police station roof and then left us in darkness again. My head throbbed as the rain began to fall in sheets, and I tried not to think of my daughter alone in that storm. I had not slept for the second night in a row.

I sat at the window and watched it storm. I was lost, too. Come home, Andi.

DAY THREE
MONDAY
MAY 17, 1999
7:30 AM

Many family members arrived from Arkansas, Oklahoma, and Kansas, and there were so many of them: my parents, of course, but also aunts, uncles, grandparents, cousins, and even kids I went to school with who I hadn't seen in years. All were there to help or offer support as best they knew how. They all came for her. People were everywhere, but I couldn't take a deep breath. I could not breathe, I could barely talk, I couldn't eat, I couldn't drink. I felt so lightheaded. However, I was so glad they were all there, but I was so out of it. In a weird way, it felt like a family reunion or a funeral. I was praying for a reunion with food, visiting, laughing, and balloons. Pink and purple were Andi's favorite colors, and we could release them to celebrate her return. What a celebration it would be. I couldn't wait for that moment.

My cousin, Jenn, was the coolest head in the storm, and she took charge of little Kristin. Melanie opted to stay with the Brewers, which, thinking back, could have been a disaster because Uncle Karl was there assisting with the search and milling around the Brewers' home, which was the second makeshift command center to the fire department.

In Mena, Hatfield, and Cove, Andi's face was everywhere in the newspaper and on television. Purple ribbons were tied around trees. Posters hung on every register at Walmart, on telephone poles, and in gas stations, jarring me into reality every time I saw them.

MISSING.

Jenn suggested we have breakfast at a local diner. Breakfast. Yuck. But I went, and we sat, and I tried to gag down some coffee. It was then we heard "local diner" talk from an adjacent booth. Two farmers were discussing the case and how if some "old boy" had taken that little girl and hurt her, they would hunt him down and kill him. It was the beginning of the disdain the community would feel against Uncle Karl that would last for many years. I couldn't even try to drink coffee after that. I wanted this nightmare to be over.

MONDAY
MAY 17, 1999
10:00 AM

Back at Greg's place in Hatfield, the site of Andi's disappearance, search and rescue had brought bloodhounds from the Oklahoma Department of Corrections. Someone told us these same animals were used in the Oklahoma City Bombing recovery. The dogs sniffed the sheets from Andi's bed and took off into the woods behind the trailer, dragging their owners behind them. My heart jumped when the dogs bayed as if they'd hit a trail, then fell short when the dogs and their owners returned without Andi.

They concluded she probably rode her four-wheeler back

there, and that was the scent they picked up. I wished they could have been there sooner. They could have picked up a trail right after she got in that godforsaken red truck...

The dogs looked up at me; their droopy faces seemed sad.

**MONDAY
MAY 17, 1999
1:00 PM**

During the chaos, I did not have much time to talk to my husband, but he finally took me by the hand and looked me deep in the eyes.

"Sit down, Rebecca; I have to talk to you about something," Kris said.

I sat on the edge of the chair and stared back at him. He hesitated, trying to find the words to say to me, then blurted them out.

"I think Karl Roberts has something to do with this."

When he said it, it sounded very foreign to me because I had not considered that possibility at all. I shook my head slowly.

"Karl would never do anything like this," I said.

Would he?

My mind rushed, and my thoughts shot through my brain, each one tripping over the one before.

He had helped in the search. He had stayed at the Brewers'

house since Andi's disappearance. For God's sake, Melanie had stayed there, too. Was she okay? Panic rose inside me. My lord, who would take a child and help with the search, then stay the night with the family?

Kris's voice was slow, measured, and careful. "I have a really bad feeling about this. I'm going to say something, and I want you to hear me out."

I sat up straight, almost challenging him. The wrong words could mean he thought she was dead, and that would be a betrayal to me.

He ran his fingers through his hair before continuing, "If Karl took her, she's dead."

Dead.

The words stung. My eyes stung. Tears streaked out of both eyes at the same time and ran down my neck. I stood up and pushed him away.

"No. She's alive, I know it. I can feel it. She's okay. Do you think I wouldn't know my own child? Do you not think I could feel if she weren't alive?"

He tried to hug me, and I stepped back further. I hated him at that moment.

I shot daggers at him with my eyes.

"How can you even consider that she might be dead?"

CHAPTER 5
THE WORST NIGHTMARE
MENA, ARKANSAS
MONDAY
MAY 17, 1999
6:30 PM

"For the thing I have greatly feared has come upon me, and what I dreaded has happened to me." Job 3:25

I have a question for you, Sheriff Oglesby. Why are you coming towards me like that with a cold, blank, terrified look that tells me more than words ever will? You look as if you are about to reach into the cage of a rattlesnake, hoping that snake won't bite you and yet knowing that it will.

You can be sure, Sheriff Oglesby, that it surely will.

Because you have not come to tell me, my little girl, Andi, has been found safe. No. You will not assure me that your deputies know where she is and that she will soon be back in my arms. I can see that your eyes are filled with the fear that only comes when one has just seen a ghost, the look of death, frigid, cruel death.

A man is behind you, Sheriff, a man who is my father, but I cannot look at him. I cannot stand the pale lips, clenched jaws, wide, scared eyes on your face. And those frightened eyes on the face of your deputy, who has slipped in behind you. They are afraid of the rattlesnake, too.

Why are they all here? My child is MISSING. She is not dead; she is missing. You all should be out looking for her, not wasting precious time here telling me things I do not want to hear, filling my head with lies I refuse to believe as truth.

Why are you removing your hat, Sheriff?

Put your goddamn hat back on.

I am an animal, an animal fighting against those who want to trap me with the truth.

Wipe those tears away from your face, Sheriff, or there will be more if I can just get to you and fight and bite like the animal I have become.

I am suffocating. Gasping for air. Short, quick, puffs.

The twenty-third Psalms pop into my head.

The Lord is my shepherd; I shall not want.

I want my daughter.

Why are you shaking your head, Sheriff? Your eyes have dropped to the floor with my stomach and my heart. Your eyes come back up and lock with mine—brave man that you are, facing a rattlesnake reared to strike. Your voice quivers.

He makes me lie down in green pastures; He leads me beside the still waters. He restores my soul; He leads me in the paths of righteousness for His name's sake.

"Rebecca, she's dead, and Karl Roberts has admitted to killing her. He's leading a team of deputies to her body now."

YEA, THOUGH I WALK THROUGH THE VALLEY OF THE SHADOW OF DEATH.

Dead. Karl Roberts. Killing. Her body.

I. WILL. FEAR. NO. EVIL.

Her body.

For you are with me.

Where are you, God?

Why God?

WHY?

Nothing. Silence.

I scream and lurch forward. The animal has broken free of the trap, but it is no good, no good because I am wounded, bleeding, dying. Then I collapse on the bed, curl in a ball, moaning in a voice that rises from the deepest part of my being. Everything is gone. Everything. Even tears. Even God.

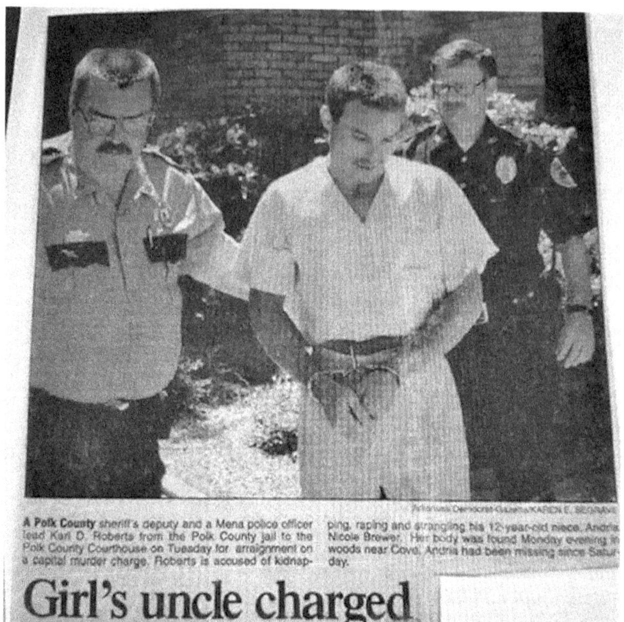

A Polk County sheriff's deputy and a Mena police officer lead Karl D. Roberts from the Polk County jail to the Polk County Courthouse on Tuesday for arraignment on a capital murder charge. Roberts is accused of kidnapping, raping and strangling his 12-year-old niece, Andria Nicole Brewer. Her body was found Monday evening in woods near Cove. Andria had been missing since Saturday.

Girl's uncle charged with capital murder

He lured her into truck, prosecutor says

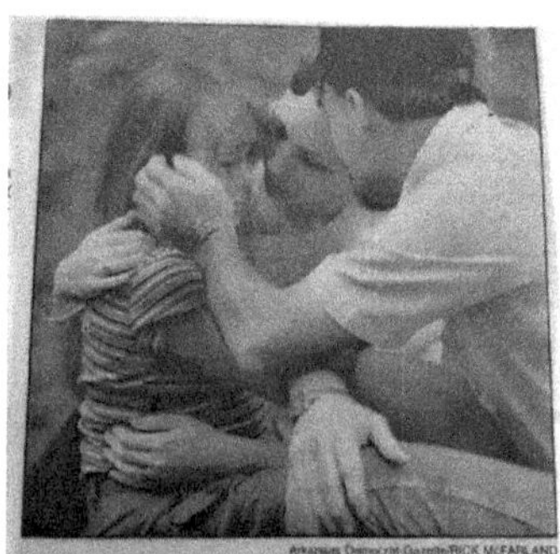

Melanie Brewer, 10, is comforted by her aunt, Kristy Griffin, and family friend Neal Taylor while waiting Monday afternoon outside her grandparents' home near Hatfield for news about the disappearance of her sister, Andria Nicole Brewer, 12. Andria has been missing since Saturday evening. Griffin is the sister of Melanie's and Andria's mother, Rebecca DeMario.

CHAPTER 6
KARL ROBERT'S WRITTEN CONFESSION
MONDAY
MAY 17, 1999
5:30 PM
ASP-CID OFFICE IN MENA
INVESTIGATOR LYNN BENEDICT'S OFFICE

On Saturday, May 15, 1999, I went to Charles Brewer's house in Hatfield at approximately 5:00 PM. I went over there to play my drums. When I got there, I took the drums outside. I turned the radio on and played along with the music. My wife and two kids were

already there. I played about an hour and a half. It took me about ten minutes to put my drums back in the room.

Then I ate dinner with the Brewers. We had salmon patties and taters. I drank tea with dinner. I had drank a six pack of Miller beer while I was playing the drums.

At about 7:45 PM, I left Charles Brewer's by myself. When I started my pickup, something hit me, I knew I was going to go by and pick up Andy (sic). I did not know if Greg was going to be home. I knew Carla was at work. About halfway up the driveway, I could see that Greg was not at home. I couldn't stop. I drove on up to the house. I got out and knocked on the front door. Andy came to the door and I told her to get in the pickup. She asked me what was wrong and I told her to just get in. We left and went straight to Cove. I didn't know where we were going, I just drove. I turned right or west at Randall's Grocery on a county road. I drove until I got to the sharp left-hand curve. The road had turned to gravel. Instead of taking the curve I went straight on a washed out clear cut road. I drove down the road a quarter of a mile or so, Andy had told me to take her home several times. The road had became grown up and I went to the right, up on a little hill. I stopped there in the road.

I told Andy to get out and she did. I got out and walked around the truck. She asked what I was going to do. I said I'm gonna fuck you. She asked me why. I told her to shut up and take your shirt off. I told her to lay down and then I took her pants off. I also took her panties off. I pulled my pants down and got on top of her. I stuck it in her, she tried to get away but I was able to hold her down. When I got through I knew I was in trouble and could not take her home. I came inside her.

I started choking her and mashing my thumbs on her throat. Her face turned blue and she went limp. I got scared and drug her over into the bushes to the right. I tried to cover her up with some old dead limbs. Before I covered her up I took her bra and shirt off. I took her clothes and put them in my pickup. I drove to the Buffalo Creek. I stopped on the wooden bridge and got her clothes out of the cab of the pickup and threw them off the right side.

Then I went to my dad's house.

ARKANSAS STATE POLICE
ASP-119
(Rev. 1/96)

Miranda Rights Form

Karl Douglass Roberts Date: 5-17-99
(First/MI/Last Name)   (Month/Day/Year)

CID - First Meth   Time: 3:16 ☐ AM ☑ PM

Before we ask you any questions, you must understand your rights.

1. Do you understand that you have the right to remain silent?

   Response: yes K. R

2. Do you understand that anything you say can and will be used against you in court?

   Response: yes K. R.

3. Do you understand that you have the right to talk to a lawyer for advice before we ask you any questions and to have him with you during questioning?

   Response: yes K R

4. Do you understand that if you cannot afford a lawyer, one will be appointed for you before any questioning if you wish, at no cost to you?

   Response: yes K R.

5. Do you understand that if you decide to answer questions now without a lawyer present, you still have the right to stop answering at any time? You also have the right to stop answering at any time until you talk to an attorney.

   Response: yes K. R.

WAIVER OF RIGHTS

I have read this statement of my rights and understand what my rights are. I am willing to make a statement and answer questions. I understand and know what I am doing. No promises or threats have been made to me and no pressure or coercion of any kind has been used against me.

Signed: Karl D. Roberts
(First/MI/Last Name)

Witness: Cpl. Dan W. Ratcliff
(Rank/First/MI/Last Name/Badge #)

up to the house. I got out and knocked on the front door. Andy came to the door and I told her to get in the pickup. She asked me what was wrong and I told her to just get in. We left and went straight to Cove. I didn't know where we were going, I just drove. I turned right or west at Randal's Grocery on a county road. I drove until I got to the sharp left hand curve. The road had turned to gravel. Instead of taking the curve I went straight on a washed out clear cut road. I drove down the road a quarter of a mile or so. Andy had told me to take her home several times. The road became narrow up and went to the right, up on a little hill. I stopped there in the road.

I told Andy to get out and she did. I got out and walked around the truck. She asked me what I was going to do. I said I'm gonna fuck you. She asked me why. I told her to shut up and take your shirt off. I told her to lay down and then I took her pants off. I also took her panties off. I pulled my pants down and got on top of her. I stuck it in her, she tried to get away but I was able to hold her down. when I got through I knew I was in trouble and I could not take her home. I came inside of her.

I started choking her and mashing my thumbs in her throat. Her face turned blue and she went limp. I got scared and drug her over into the bushes to the right. I tried to cover her up with some old dead limbs. Before I covered her up I took her bra and skirt off.

I took her clothes and put them in my pickup. I drove to Buffalo creek and threw her clothes in the creek. I stopped on the wooden bridge and got her clothes out of the cab of the pickup and threw them off of the right side. The I went to my Dad's house. K.R.

6:54 p.m. 5-12-99

Karl Roberts

Inv. Ottie V. Ratcliff
2A Mark A. Jessie - FBI 5/17/99

CHAPTER 7
MORE THAN HER DEMISE

Left to Right: Andi & Memaw – Andi & Papa Taylor

Papa Petty & Andi

CHAPTER 8
THE AFTERMATH
MONDAY
MAY 17, 1999
9:30 AM

Everyone wanted comfort. I had none to give. I passed through a sea of eyes, eyes full of pain, looking to me for answers, for strength. And there were many eyes offering comfort in my direction. I could not receive it. It was as if I were in a bubble, behind a wall that I had erected to protect myself. No one in, no one out.

About an hour after we found out about Andi, I saw my mother. She approached me. Her eyes, wide and brown—full of pain. I could not let her look at me. I could not hear her voice. Only she could break the bubble, and I wasn't ready for it to be broken. Not yet. I put a hand up to shield those eyes and put a finger to her lips to signal silence. She flinched away from my hand, not understanding.

I did it again. "Sh! Don't say anything to me, don't say

anything!"

She didn't. She reached out and cradled me in her arms, and I was her baby once again.

After my mom released me from her embrace, four-year-old Kristin came running up to us, blowing the bubbles Aunt Jenn had bought her and said, "Memaw, did you know Andi died and went to heaven, and now she's with Jesus?"

My mom and I melted into a hug for her. There was wailing and weeping elsewhere behind us, a sense of being lost. I felt flushed and hot; I was going to throw up. I jumped up and ran for the toilet. I fell on my knees in front of the bowl and began to heave. At first, nothing came up, but the heaving was so hard that I could barely stop to breathe. Yellow bile rose in my throat, reminding me that I hadn't eaten in days, but I couldn't stop dry heaving.

Heave. Stars. Heave. Stars. Heave. Stars.

My face was red and sweaty, perspiration rolling down my neck. Someone laid a cool washcloth on the back of my neck. This stopped the heaving, and I was helped up. I lay down on the bed. I just needed a few minutes to process it.

Oh my God, my girl was gone. I was down for the count; I just wanted to lie there and never move again. My head throbbed, and my body ached. People were still milling all over the place, so I got back up. I saw my friend, Cassie, from high school, and she handed me a basket with a plant and a ceramic angel. She barely had words but told me she had looked all over the county for Andi. It meant more to me than she realized. Not only was life sucked out of me, but I could tell life had been sucked out of the community.

The small-town rumor mill had, by this time, become a beast of its own. I heard rumors of psychics who claimed they helped police find her. People whispered that Andi had been a satanic sacrifice and had been dismembered (not true), and others mumbled that she enticed Uncle Karl and indicated she had it coming. These were awful untruths that were very painful to all of us who loved her—love her.

An hour and a half after finding out about Andi, a call came from Colleen Nick, whose daughter, Morgan, had been abducted by a stranger and never returned four years prior. I took the call and could barely speak because I was crying too hard. During the entire three-day ordeal, I desperately needed to talk to someone who understood what I was going through. Someone who had walked in my shoes. I remembered the story of her daughter being taken from a Little League baseball game, and I only knew her from the widespread news coverage. Four years ago, I had held Andi and Melanie tighter at the thought of something so tragic happening to them. Andi and Melanie had been very frightened after the abduction of Morgan Nick.

Now, I was the mother, crying on the news. Begging. Colleen was like a breath of fresh air when I heard her voice. The intimate conversation was met with tears on both ends. She prayed for me and my family. She cried with me over our little girls. She also offered to have someone else reach out to me, Marc Klaas, whose 12-year-old daughter, Polly, had been abducted, raped, and strangled in Petaluma, California. I told her I would like to talk to him—any ally in a storm. We said our goodbyes, and I placed the phone in the cradle.

I was numb.

There was a knock on the door. I stood up and opened it. A ginger-haired man and a tall brunette woman stood there. I did not know them. Before I could say anything, he introduced himself.

"Ma'am, my name is Tim Williamson. I am the prosecutor for the 18th West Judicial District in the state of Arkansas. This is

JoAnn Mitchell, my victim witness coordinator; she is here to help you. I am so sorry for your loss, but I want to make sure you know that in the morning at 9:00 AM, we will be arraigning Mr. Roberts at the Polk County Courthouse for the crime of capital murder. I'd like you to come to my office at 8:00 AM so we can talk for a few minutes before we go to court. This will not take long, but we want to prepare you for what will happen in the court proceeding."

He handed me his card. I looked at it.

"Again, I am so sorry for your loss."

I stared into his face. I said nothing, only took his card and shut the door.

I was on my knees in front of the toilet again after they left.

Heave.

Stars.

Heave.

Stars.

**TUESDAY
MAY 18, 1999
8:00 AM**

The next morning, I found myself in the Office of the Prosecuting Attorney along with other members of our family. Prosecutor Williamson and JoAnn Mitchell entered the room.

"Please come to my office." His southern drawl was thick. I did as he said—I was still an injured animal, though I wasn't sure he realized it.

With no bedside manner whatsoever, he began, "I have decided not to charge him with the abduction of your daughter. I believe the rape and murder charge is enough to warrant capital murder."

I gasped and tried to gulp in air. I needed a paper bag; I was beginning to hyperventilate. I turned in a circle, meeting the eyes of each family member standing in the room.

Rape?

Rape?

Did they all know she had been raped and had forgotten to tell me? Their eyes told me they did not know because they were all looking at each other as well. Through all of this, it had never entered my mind that Andi might have been raped. I was naïve about some things. I was just a mom who took her kids to church and worked as a preschool teacher so I could be off work when my kids were home. I was trying to be the perfect wife and mother. It was as though I was standing before the sheriff, and he was telling me she was dead all over again. This time, however, I was no rattlesnake— the injured animal had succumbed to its injuries. I was broken. Dead inside. My knees gave out, and they hit the floor too hard. I didn't pass out. My legs just stopped working. I couldn't explain it; it had never happened to me before or since. Tears began to flow, and I grabbed hold of my face and wept.

Kris raised his voice. Something about being more sensitive and how we didn't know she had been raped.

I heard the prosecutor apologize; his voice seemed muffled. Someone helped me up, and I walked out back to the alleyway to get some fresh air. The warm spring day had the birds chirping. The day was perfect, with blue skies and a gentle wind. I couldn't comprehend how the weather could be this perfect when my world was burning down.

We walked back inside the prosecutor's office, and he began again more gently. He positioned JoAnn next to me.

"Karl Douglas Roberts will be arraigned at 9:00 this morning and charged with first-degree capital murder. He will not receive bail. He will more than likely plead not guilty, but that means nothing. The state will prove otherwise, and this case will go to a jury trial. I highly suspect Mr. Roberts will receive the death penalty. He will never be a free man again."

He may as well have been speaking Chinese to me because I heard "death penalty" and "will never be a free man." That's it. I knew nothing of the criminal justice process. In fact, I was so sheltered I really didn't even know what a prosecutor did. But, oh, how I would learn in the coming months and years.

We were whisked inside the Polk County Courthouse, where

a quick arraignment charged Karl with first-degree capital murder, and he pleaded "not guilty," as expected.

Funny. He didn't look like the devil. He looked completely and utterly normal.

His actions had warranted him the name "Devil." He stood in front of the judge dressed in jailhouse orange, and the only thing I could think was: DEVIL killed my daughter. He killed her. With his hands, those weapons of flesh.

Clean-cut hair. Short, well-kept nails. Bulletproof vest. We had learned he had received many death threats. He had a scratch across the top of his nose and down onto his cheek. Andi had fought him. I knew it. He offered no eye contact, just kept his gaze down. The deputies who had marched him into the courtroom in handcuffs whisked him out as soon as he was charged. And that was that. Short and quick.

The next thing I remembered was standing outside the courthouse. Reporters surrounded me, asking if I wanted to make a comment.

I shook my head. "No."

All I could think of was that I had a funeral to plan for a 12-year-old girl.

I put the bubble back up.

CHAPTER 9
FUNERAL ARRANGEMENTS

By late morning, many more of our friends and family had begun to arrive from out of state, filling up most of the hotels in the small town of Mena, Arkansas. Friends and townsfolk comforted as best they could. Everyone was incredibly sad. Our close friends from the Tulsa area traveled to assist us in case we needed something. They took care of crowd control, ran interference with the media, tried to get me to eat, stop crying, and helped with the kids. We received an increasing number of calls and messages from people who wanted to send flowers and donate money.

A benevolent fund was established at a local bank, and the flower shops in Mena were inundated with orders for flower arrangements for the upcoming funeral. They had to call in all their extra help. Many flower orders were placed from out of state, but an enormous amount came from people who lived in Arkansas—strangers whom Andi's story had touched.

I called Greg to be part of the funeral arrangements and asked him to meet me at the funeral home. He agreed.

I was waiting in the parking lot of the funeral home later that afternoon when Greg pulled his car up next to me and rolled the window down. I could tell he wasn't doing very well. He stared straight ahead; his eyes were dark with circles underneath, and his hands shook.

"I can't do it," he said. "I—can—not—plan—her—funeral."

I stared at him for a moment, not really understanding what he was saying.

"There is no choice, park your car, we have to."

But then he did something that shocks me still to this day.

"No," he said. He rolled up his window, gave the car a little gas, causing the tires to slip on the gravel, and drove away. In my mind, he peeled out, but really, he didn't; it just seemed that way.

I stared at the back of his vehicle as it pulled out onto the highway and headed south back toward Hatfield. I was wide-eyed, slack-jawed.

At that moment, I decided I would not let my grief be so great that I couldn't attend to my daughter's last bit of business on this earth. My stomach gnawed as flashes of guilt ran through me, reminding me that it was partially my fault that, at that very second, she was at the medical examiner's office in Little Rock being autopsied.

An autopsy!

It was me who allowed her to move to this hellhole. I wanted a do-over. Isn't that in the parenting manual—that you get a mulligan?

It was then that I shifted my thinking. I forced the playing field to change. As her father drove away, the second time that week, I turned around and faced the door. I looked at the signage, Hall Funeral Service, and reached out to put my hand on the door. It was cold.

Cold.

I pulled the door open and entered the building. The funeral director stood there with an outstretched hand. I wanted to punch him in the mouth; instead, I placed my hand in his—it was very warm. He squeezed and introduced himself.

"Please come into my office."

His office, not much unlike the Prosecuting Attorney's office, seemed sterile and official. The oak desk had his name plaque with a slot for his business cards, and a peace lily thrived on the corner. Behind him was a display of urns, and on the wall to the left was a photograph of his family smiling. I couldn't bear to look at it for long; happiness felt like an illusion to me now. We made small talk, and he offered his condolences, mentioning that she was at the Chief Medical Examiner's office and would be back by Thursday. I told him I knew that already, but I didn't remember who had told me. I wondered who arranged all this for my child—the trip to Little Rock, the medical procedures they were performing on her. It was as though I didn't matter anymore; I was the collateral damage that had to be dealt with for them to do what had to be done. I tried to regroup; I felt like I was going crazy. I had to get out of my own head. It wasn't a pretty place to be right now.

I picked out the flyers that would be passed out at the funeral—pink with a bouquet of flowers. And I arranged her funeral. Nothing can be said about arranging the funeral of your child except it is the pain of all pains. A dagger in the heart.

REVELATION

God hath not promised
Skies always blue,
Flower-strewn pathways
All our lives through;
God hath not promised
Sun without rain,
Joy without sorrow,
Peace without pain.

But God hath promised
Strength for the day,
Rest for the labor,
Light for the way
Grace for the trials,
Help from above.
Unfailing sympathy,
Undying love. . .

And God shall wipe away all tears
from their eyes

Revelation 21:4

In Loving Memory

Andria Nichole Brewer

Born
Friday April 10, 1987

Passed Away
Saturday May 15, 1999

Services Held At
Hatfield First Baptist Church
May 22, 1999
10:00 AM

Conducted By
Pastor Arvie Knight

Concluding Service
Six Mile Cemetery
Hatfield, AR

Arrangements By
Hall Funeral Service, Inc.
Mena, AR

Missing. Murdered. Funeral preparation. I knew it would get worse, but at that moment, it was the worst thing I had ever experienced. Actual hell would probably have been a relief.

"Now for the hard part," the funeral director said.

Really? Because ALL of this had been pretty fucking hard.

The casket selection. Of course, this would be a literal nail in my own coffin.

I followed the funeral director down a long corridor. He cracked open a door, put his hand inside to turn on the light, and swung the door open.

It looked like a room in a spook house, caskets displayed from wall to wall. I knew any moment Dracula would sit up out of one of those things. I swallowed hard, took a deep breath, and stepped past him.

I immediately spotted the casket for Andi—a pastel pink one. Inside, a soft white satin pillow with ruffles.

I pointed at it and said, "I want that one for her. It's pretty."

I wanted to puke.

I hate you, Karl Roberts.

Devil.

For the first time in my life, I knew what it truly felt like to hate.

THURSDAY
MAY 20, 1999

Thursday morning, the funeral director called and notified us that Andi's body had been returned from the crime lab in Little Rock. When I arrived at the funeral home, the funeral director told me that I could go to the room at the end of the hall where she was "resting."

The overwhelming smell of flowers was sweet and putrid. It left a bad, heavy taste in my mouth, like the aftertaste of a diet soda. I slowly peeked around the corner to the flower-lined foyer. Bouquets spilled out of the room. The funeral director, noticing my curiosity about the flowers, said, "All of these flowers are Andi's. We have had to use another entire viewing room; there are so many we didn't have room for them all in one room."

I offered a weak smile.

I took a step toward the room Andi was in. I could hear my heart pounding. I didn't want to go in. I wanted to run away. The swooshing sound in my ears was deafening. I entered the room. The casket I had picked out sat there in all its grandiose pastel pink. A mountain of flowers was stacked to the ceiling. I slowly walked over to her closed casket and ran my hand over the smooth top.

I had asked if we could have an open casket.

"I'm sorry, no, the elements had gotten to her."

A nice way of saying your daughter had rotted beyond repair in the humid southern heat.

I could see now why some people passed out in front of the casket of a loved one. I shook off the woozy feeling and continued rubbing the casket. Her picture sat on top, and as soon as I looked at it, I started to cry.

"I'm sorry. I'm so sorry." I repeated that over and over. I couldn't stop saying it.

The tears refused to stop, so I just stood there and cried and said I was sorry. It wasn't my finest moment. I didn't know how long I stood there. It was a long while.

CHAPTER 10
THE FUNERAL
SATURDAY
MAY 22, 1999

I put on my blue dress and looked in the mirror. I didn't know the woman staring back at me. Was it possible that the events of one single week could destroy a person? A family?

The humidity was high, and my hair was limp. My bangs hung in my eyes. I brushed them aside.

Don't be a scaredy cat, Andi...

Did I say that to a child? What was wrong with me? Thinking that I could have been responsible for leaving that little girl with one ounce of fear in her short life was a crushing burden. I should have let her sleep with me that night; I shouldn't have been such a selfish fool.

I didn't like the woman I saw in the mirror. Look at me, dressing for my daughter's funeral, all hope lost. Putting on a blue dress I had gotten from the half-price rack at Dillard's, trying to fix hair that was impossible—I looked too pale. Heart in a million pieces. Stomach-churning. I seriously hated myself.

We made the ride to the church in silence. I felt so alone. This was my journey, my road. Comfort was offered, but I rejected it, like the hell I was enduring was the price I had to pay for being a shitty mother who had allowed her daughter to move away. This was my fault. If I had told her no, she would be alive.

When we arrived, the parking lot was packed. The Arkansas State Police were directing traffic off the highway. The Polk County Sheriff's Department was there; the news media had cameras set up on the side of the road and filmed us as we turned in. It was so hot. Sweat slipped down my back.

We walked into the church and waded through a vast number of people in the vestibule. We joined our family and the Brewer family in the large dining area to wait until the service began. The next thing I knew, we were being escorted into the sanctuary. I noticed the cross of Christ hanging at the front of the church above the Baptismal—an empty cross that signified a living God. A living God who apparently ignored children being raped in the woods. My breath caught in my throat for having such a blasphemous thought. I was not raised to disrespect the Almighty in His own house, but I was clearly having irrational thoughts and glanced up at the ceiling, waiting for the lightning. When it didn't come, a lonely feeling settled upon me, and even though the church was packed to standing room only, it was as though I was the only one there. People were lined up outside the doors and standing in the parking lot. Yet, I was still alone, just like in the final moments when I pushed this child out of my body and realized that this birthing thing was all on me. I had to give the final push to give her life. No one else could do it for me. Like this, no one could do this for me either. The big difference was that giving birth to her left me with the reward of holding her in my arms; this would be taking her away forever.

I did a visual sweep of the congregation and recognized many people from our church in Oklahoma. My entire family was there. Everything seemed to be moving in slow motion. I heard wailing and realized it was me. Melanie was in a bright yellow dress. It was the brightest yellow I had ever seen, like the sun. Everyone was dressed in bright spring colors because I told them not to wear black; she wouldn't have wanted that. Maybe I couldn't look into a black abyss any more than I already had.

I looked to my right and observed my mom and stepdad entering the sanctuary. She had her arms around him, almost carrying him. He was crying harder than I had ever seen him cry. I thought back to when I told him I was pregnant with Andi, how he had expressed disappointment in me. Yet, when Andi was born, they immediately bonded. Both my mom and stepfather loved her so much. I had given her to all these people, and I had played my part in taking her away. The guilt of letting her move crushed my soul again.

My pastor from Oklahoma took the platform and stated that this was the hardest funeral he had ever been asked to preach. He looked very odd standing in a church that wasn't his own, looming above that pastel pink casket. I thought about all the church plays Andi had performed in and wondered if, in such a large church congregation with so many kids running around, he even remembered which one she was. But he did. He truly honored Andi and her life beautifully. In the middle of the service, Pastor read a poem written by one of Andi's classmates, and there wasn't a dry eye in the church.

"Amazing Grace," "Lion and the Lamb," and *"My Redeemer Lives,"* performed by Andi's favorite singer, Crystal Lewis, were played over the church sound system. I cried again. I placed my head in my hands. The physical toll hurt emotionally and physically.

When the funeral was over, I looked at Andi's father, Greg. I saw her in him, always had. However, he looked as though he had aged 20 years. Did I look this bad? Probably. Pain was etched deeply in his face. I walked over to him. We embraced and cried together. The tears we shed for our daughter were one.

Finally, I walked outside and was handed a pink balloon. When everyone had a balloon, we all released them. I watched as they drifted out of sight, becoming tiny dots in the sky and then vanishing.

I'm sorry. I'm so sorry.

The guilt was crushing.

On the way to the car, a young police officer from the Arkansas State Police approached us. He was crying, trembling. He removed his hat, nodded, and said, "This is for you, ma'am." He placed a brown teddy bear dressed as a state patrolman in my hands.

"Thank you," I said.

We were filmed for the news as we drove the curvy single-lane road toward the cemetery, leading a long procession. Andi's funeral was the top story on the news in Fort Smith, Little Rock, and Baton Rouge that evening.

A tragic ending to a three-day statewide search for a 12-year-old girl from Polk County, Arkansas...

At the cemetery, the funeral director led us to our seats in front of the casket. The sun blazed down hard, and the green funeral tent sucked up the heat, making it feel like we were in a sauna. The pastor gave a mini-sermon, people paid their respects, and the crowd gradually dispersed. I sat in a metal folding chair in front of my daughter's pink casket. I wanted to crawl inside the casket and be buried with her. I didn't want to live life this way.

Kris wanted to leave to pick up Kristin and Kristofer, who hadn't attended the funeral and had stayed in Mena with the victim-witness coordinator, Jo. I told him to go on, and he did. I felt resentful that he so easily left me there, alone, but didn't have the energy to raise an argument.

After a little while, I watched them lower my beautiful 12-year-old daughter into the ground—the baby I had had while I was still a baby, the one I taught to walk and talk, who had the most infectious giggle I had ever heard and the most beautiful hands I had ever seen. The girl who loved her cat named Peanut Butter and Jelly because she said she looked like a peanut butter and jelly sandwich. The girl who played basketball and rode her four-wheeler, who wore lip gloss and smarted off like any other kid, had left a crater-sized hole in my heart. I closed my eyes as the last little bit of pastel pink disappeared below ground.

Sheriff Deputy Bailey watched me witness the lowering and realized that I was in trouble. Nausea flooded over me like a wave, and I felt the need to heave. He pulled me up by my elbow, put his hand around my waist, and steered me toward his police vehicle, where he helped me inside the cruiser. He turned the air on full blast cold and pointed it in my face.

"Put your head down and breathe," he said. He knew. He had probably seen his share of grieving mothers in his twenty-year career in law enforcement, though he later admitted that he had never been a part of anything like this. He rushed me back to the church and brought me a glass of water and a cool cloth to put on the back of my neck. I sat waiting for Kris to come back with the kids. Eventually, he showed back up. I just wanted to go home. We rode back to Oklahoma in silence.

CHAPTER 11
OKLAHOMA
DAYS LATER...

I struggled for normalcy, but it was gone, seemingly for good. I didn't know what to do. Though my world was wrecked, everyone else went on with their lives much as if nothing had happened—except when they saw me. Then, most made a wide swath around me or struggled for words to say. It was insane because I was still me. I was not different. Yet, I had become a leper of sorts. Loneliness enveloped me; no one understood. I just wanted to feel better, to be the person I was, but I couldn't. It was gone. She was gone. I was gone.

As time crawled, my heart longed for answers. They said time healed all pain, but I stood in disagreement with that statement. There was no possible way anything could fix this. Even so, I craved justice, but I was ignorant of the process, and it had only been a few weeks. This way of life was foreign to me. I hated it; I hated feeling like my heart was an empty shell. I hated waking up in the morning with the sun touching my face, opening my eyes, and remembering that I was now in hell. I hated the feeling of a lead block dropping into my stomach. I wanted my old life.

Justice seemed so far away. I did not know what was going to happen. I knew nothing about the criminal justice system. Finally, some answers arrived in an off-white envelope. I opened it slowly and unfolded it. In the margin on the left was a shadowed image of a young girl I presumed to be Polly Klaas; the letter was from her father, Marc. Polly had been abducted at knifepoint in 1993 from her Petaluma, California home, raped, and strangled. I held Marc's letter in my hands and began to read:

Like you, I am the parent of a lovely child kidnapped and murdered by a predatory monster.

Like you, I have cried, grieved, and had trouble finding reasons to go on living.

The victimization is not over. You must now face the criminal justice system and all that it represents. Remember, as you prepare for trial, all the rights belong to the killer. He has a lawyer. You do not; the prosecutor represents the state. You and your daughter are merely the currency that fuels the criminal justice system. He has the right to a change of venue, the right to appeal, and the right to act out in court. You have none of these rights. His lawyer only has to convince one juror of his potential innocence; the prosecutor has to convince all twelve of his guilt. This sounds grim, and it is.

This was awful. Yet he ended with a small glimmer of hope that Andi could never be hurt again and that she sat on my shoulder and whispered, *"Go, Mom, go."*

I felt thankful for his letter yet dreaded what was coming.

How does a person—a mother, a father—survive this? Grief beat on me with its angry fists of hate.

What was happening?

I decided to focus on the short term and just breathe. Just make it to the next breath, the next moment. I sat in the living room and looked at the television. SpongeBob was yelling at Patrick. My daughters were sitting cross-legged on the floor, laughing.

I was not.

JUNE 1999

The phone rang. It was Colleen Nick. I felt a bond with her since she was the first person I had talked to after I found out Andi had been murdered. She invited our family to One Hope, an event to honor and bring awareness to her missing daughter, Morgan. This year, they were releasing thousands of pink balloons with photos and information about Morgan tied to each one. Large banners representing missing children from across the nation would be plastered all around the Alma, Arkansas, football stadium. There would be several different banners: one with the names of missing children, one with the names of children who had been internationally abducted, one with the names of runaways, one for Morgan, and one with the names of children who had been kidnapped and murdered. Colleen asked if it would be okay to put Andi's name on the banner for kidnapped and murdered children. I said yes.

Was this how it all ends?

I also told Colleen we would come. She was surprised, but I didn't know what else to do. I felt I had to do something. A nervousness had been riding on me since we got back to Oklahoma. I had felt tired and grouchy and needed to do something with my hands. My fingernails were all but gone.

My family arrived at the stadium that first Saturday in June, welcomed with open arms by the staff of the Morgan Nick Foundation, the organization Colleen started shortly after Morgan's abduction. I spotted Colleen amidst the thousands of helium-filled balloons, recognizing her from her frequent appearances on the nightly news. She walked straight to me, and I was lost in her embrace. An overwhelming sense that she completely understood enveloped me like a warm wind. We stood there and cried. It was unlike anything I had ever experienced; she got me, she got it. She had walked in my shoes. God help us both.

I glanced beyond her, and in the center of the football stadium, ten thousand pink balloons waited to be released.

The ceremony began, and Colleen took the stage. She spoke of her daughter in a way I had never heard anyone speak about a loved one. It was foreign yet beautiful. She spoke of how special Morgan was to everyone, of how Morgan wanted to be a circus performer and a doctor. I felt so sad that Morgan was taken; I prayed for her to come home. And then I prayed for Andi. I didn't even know why I prayed for her—it was too late for her—but I did it anyway. I heard someone weeping and turned around; my whole family was crying, but it was my sister, Kristy, whose weeping I had heard.

A newspaper reporter snapped a picture of us, and they put it on the front page of the Sunday morning newspaper in Fort Smith.

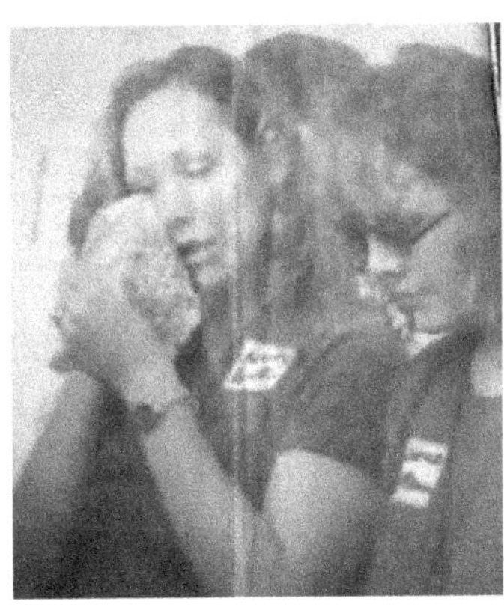

The net holding the balloons was pulled, and they rose, peppering the sky. It was a phenomenal sight. They ascended into the air, and at about 2,000 feet, they formed the perfect shape of a pink heart. Then, the heart parted in half and whirled upward, slipping from sight.

Afterward, we walked down to the display board honoring the children, and I saw my daughter's name on the abducted and murdered board. Another sour reminder that I would never see Andi again, never hear her giggle—that dut, dut, dut high-pitched sound she launched when something was funny.

Feeling the need to escape, my family and I left Alma, Arkansas, the next morning and headed for Branson, Missouri. We rented a cabin on Lake Taneycomo. The kids were excited about the trip but clearly exhausted, and there was a quietness about them. They didn't fight on the long drive to Missouri; they just sat silently in the back seat. Kris and I made small talk. I wasn't sure we would ever recover and be what we were before. None of us would.

We checked into a small cabin and decided to take a walk along the bank of the river. It was quiet and cool, not many people around because it was the middle of the week. I breathed in the fresh, crisp air blowing off the lake, saw a trout jump, and heard the birds sing, but I was not me. We found an old playground, and the kids played while we watched from a nearby bench.

"I don't know what to do," I said to Kris.

"There is nothing we can do."

A man on the corner began to play his guitar. We sat there for what seemed like an eternity, listening to him strum old church hymns and James Taylor songs while the kids played.

We spent the next two weeks trying to make sense of it all. I felt desperate, as if hope was gone from the world. The murderer had killed a part of me. My family was no longer complete. The days of spending time together were gone, and although we were going through the motions of living, it wasn't the same. Each night in Branson, I put the kids to bed around ten o'clock and then sat outside the cabin in an old white lawn chair. I took up the habit of chain-smoking Swisher Sweets until the wee hours of the morning. The pit in my stomach wouldn't go away. The torment of what Andi had gone through haunted me. I was going crazy; my mind wouldn't shut off. And then the nightmares began.

I am in my childhood bedroom in Wichita, Kansas. Dennis Rader, the BTK Strangler, is on the loose, and I am frightened, much like when I was a child.

I see a shadowy figure, a man, at the window.

Bind you. Torture you. Kill you.

I run into the living room, and Andi's open pink casket is sitting in front of me. I don't want to see her face; no, don't make me look at her face. I fight by grabbing onto the door facing. My feet won't stop. They pull me to the open lid. The shadowy image throws its hands onto a window and shouts, "Becca, hurry up and feed the corpse." I try to close the lid of the casket, but I see her face. Lips blue, face white, eyes sewn shut. Then, her body begins to convulse. Hands and feet thrashing up and down. Feet kicking the lower half of the coffin, hands reaching, trying to push up and out mid-convulse.

"Mommy, help me."

Bind.

Torture.

Kill.

My eyes flew open, my chest heaving; I woke up in a pool of sweat, gasping for air. I had not thought of my childhood boogeyman, BTK, in many years, but here he was, back to haunt my dreams, pulled from the depths of my brain to remind me that Karl Roberts was not the only boogeyman I had ever experienced. Growing up in Wichita, Kansas, had haunted my soul since childhood.

Hello. I'm back. And I brought a friend. His name is Uncle Karl.

I got up, went to the bathroom, washed my face, grabbed the smokes, and sat down in the white lawn chair. It was 4 AM. I listened to the frogs chirping, the creatures of the night, an owl hooting, the shroud of darkness. I pulled on the small cigar and let my mind take me back in time. Every time I closed my eyes, I dreamed of Karl Roberts and BTK. I couldn't shake it. I would never be okay.

WICHITA, KS
MAY 1975

My mother's eyes were wide like a doe in the headlights of an oncoming vehicle.

"He said it meant 'Bind them, torture them, kill them.' What kind of person said that? What kind of person did that?" she whispered.

My father, clearly shaken, swiveled his head back and forth as he pulled into our driveway and snapped off the radio. They had just heard the latest news report on a purported murderous fiend haunting our city of roughly 280,000. The green 1971 Ford F-250 lunged slightly forward as my father rammed it into park in the driveway of our small, modest home.

"Stay here with your sister," he said. "We'll be right back." My parents hopped out of the cab of the truck, leaving us alone.

I sat there as wide-eyed as a five-year-old girl could be, my fingers reaching over to grasp my little sister Kristy's pudgy hand as the console light dimmed. She was eighteen months old and didn't understand what was happening, so she sat there watching as our mother walked into our home on Sandy Street. Then, she averted her eyes to watch our father disappear behind the house. My sister's free hand began to twist a curl on the side of her towhead. She puckered out her bottom lip.

"Don't cry, sissy. It's okay," I lied. But I knew she was about to cry because our mother was out of sight; she was too young to understand that the situation was more dire than our mother slipping out of sight. She didn't know what I knew because I listened in the shadows where the adults did not see me. I heard them, and I silently sat crouched behind a door or in the hallway, absorbing every word. I could tell by the higher pitch of their voices that something was bad. I listened to them talk of death and mayhem. How the whole city was on edge. How there was a madman on the loose. How things like this weren't supposed to happen in Wichita, Kansas. How he killed people, how first he cut the phone line and then hid in their home, waiting. Like a monster. A real monster, not like in the movies, oh no, much worse. And it was rumored that he waited for hours. Waiting like an animal crouched in the bushes for its prey. Except he wasn't waiting for a meal. He was waiting for his own sick killing pleasure. He smothered them and choked them or hanged them from the basement rafters. He bound them, he tortured them, then he killed them. He wanted to be called the BTK. I didn't fully understand the concept of all that was happening, but I knew it was not good. My father checked the back of the house to make sure the phone line wasn't cut, and my mother checked the house to make sure there was a dial tone on our rotary phone. Why?

Kristy let out a whimper. I squeezed her hand tighter. I saw a single tear drop out of her eye. Did she feel my fear? I didn't think so and prayed she didn't understand.

But I did.

The words quadruple homicide danced around. The two words sounded so foreign. Big words. Words too big for a young girl, but I remembered them because they had a ring to them—quadruple homi-cide. Not fully certain what it meant, but I understood that my mommy and daddy were on edge. Now, when we came back from visiting my grandparents, or anywhere for that matter, especially after dark, this routine of them checking the house had become commonplace. It was then that Kristy and I were left in the car alone.

Alone. In the dark.

To wait while they checked to make sure the coast was clear. And what was I supposed to do if they never came back? What if the door to the house slammed with my mother inside or my father never came around from the backyard? They never told me what to do if they didn't come back. So, I hung on to the pudgy hand of my sister and stuck my thumbnail in my mouth and chewed. Gnawing furiously. I could hear my heart beating in my ears.

Swoosh. Swoosh. Swoosh.

"Please come back, please come back, please come back."

It was then that I saw my mother's head pop out the front door. She gave the all-clear about the time my father appeared from the back of our blue house.

"Phone line is good; we are good."

I dropped my sister's hand as she began to wail for Mother. Mom rushed to her, and I let out a heavy sigh. That night, we had been spared the wrath of a demon.

Being raised in Wichita, Kansas, had its moments of living in a total nightmare. I was always a little nervous about having a dial tone on the phone, often picking up the phone and slowly raising it to my ear, eyes wide, heart racing; only hearing the hum of the tone made my pulse slow down. I was always afraid to go to the basement. I was instantly petrified when I heard the whispering of the name BTK.

Perhaps his killing spree happened at a very influential time in my youthful development while I was growing up. BTK was never far from our lips when the Kansas sun melted down the horizon. There was always a group of us neighbor kids who would play outside a little after dark. We would play spooky games with the boogeyman as the centerpiece of our terror.

"BTK is coming for you," one neighborhood boy would chant. "Let's play hide and seek. You have to hide and make a run for the porch. I am BTK. One, two, three, now go!"

I took off running and hid in the line of evergreen trees beside our home. My hair got tangled in the sap of the tree, and the smell of the rich earth spiraled around my face. I hid, barely breathing.

And I was terrified.

"Ready or not, here I come," the boy yelled. And the look on his face seemed pure evil. In my mind's eye, he looked possessed as he came after us.

The rational part of me knew he was just a kid from up the block. But part of me knew a killer was on the loose, and the fact that we were outside after dark played tricks on my mind. As I stayed covered in the branches of that old evergreen, with my breath coming in short puffs, I waited until he got out of sight, looking for the other kids. My hiding spot was superb. When he rounded the corner, I sprinted. The glow of the porch light seemed a million miles away. My long, skinny legs dug in. He must have heard me because he reappeared from around the corner.

"I see you." What I saw was a monster with a rope around his neck, purple face, and strangling.

The globe covering the porch light grew larger as I approached our house; it bounced up and down with every footstep. I smelled the chicken that was cooking inside coming through the porch screen. I was screaming when I tried to run up the stairs of the porch, and the boogeyman barely missed me. I sprawled out spread eagle and caught both of my knees on the top step. I didn't even care as the throb of pain hit me full throttle. I was safe.

"Shit, you're home free," he said, and his face changed from the monster to the neighbor kid from up the street.

I rolled over to my back, realizing that he had used profanity and my mother was standing at the door with her hands on her hips. I knew she was going to tell his mother, and he'd probably get a spanking.

"What exactly is going on here?"

"He scared me; I thought he was BTK."

"Go home, Johnny. It's getting late. Your mom is gonna wonder where you are. Look at those knees, Becc. Get in here."

The horror of growing up as a latchkey kid in a town with a serial killer kept flooding my thoughts as it seemed that BTK and Roberts were the same demon that had followed me my entire life. Why, I wondered, was it me who was cursed, or was evil just everywhere?

I took a long pull of the Swisher; the cherry glowed in the dark, and I slowly exhaled a puff of white smoke. Thinking back to the days when I was plagued with night terrors made my stomach flop. Such fear, such real nightmares that I would wake up screaming. One night, I screamed so violently that my folks had to take me to the emergency room; the nightmares, much like the one I had just had about Andi, I prayed they weren't coming back to stay. BTK had caught me in my dreams the night of the emergency room visit, and I didn't snap out of it until the doctor grabbed me by the shoulders and shouted my name, not Becca, but REBECCA. When I snapped out of it, I started to cry, and my mother gathered me into her arms.

I prayed and smoked. I prayed for Andi again; maybe I just wanted to make sure God realized she was there with him, and I prayed the nightmares were not coming back.

The trip to Branson wasn't what I would call a vacation. I longed for home again.

CHAPTER 12
FALL 1999

The nightmares became regular. I craved sleep, but not the nightmares that accompanied it. And I was so pissed at God. I didn't act mad outwardly, but inside, a storm brewed. I even faked it by going to church and pretending that I was okay. I wasn't. I hated the word victim. I hated that I felt guilty when I laughed. I hated the dropping sensation in my stomach. I hated the way people at church looked at me like I was a pitiful little thing. I hated when people told me things like, "You have an angel watching over you," and "Aren't you glad you have other children?" But what I hated most was, "You are so strong; I could never survive what you are going through." Like I was supposed to kill myself or something? I had no choice. This was it. The shitty hand I had been dealt. Now, what was I going to do with it?

I tried praying and "giving it up" to the Lord. But I was met with silence. Was this God thing even real? I had been raised to believe, without reservation, that Jesus is the Son of God and is a living entity. He would never leave or forsake me. Blah, blah, blah. However, I felt forsaken and alone. Flashes of Andi being forsaken and alone overtook my mind. I tried to be faithful, but I lost my desire to go to church. It made me nauseous to think about walking into that building and listening to Pastor preach about how everything was going to be alright. I just couldn't handle it, so I stopped attending church altogether. I couldn't be part of the Sunday-Sunday night-Wednesday night choir crowd anymore. It was too much to handle when all I could concentrate on was the pre-trial hearing for the capital murder case scheduled for the fall of 1999.

Greg called me in September and told me that Andi's headstone had been set on her grave at Six-Mile Cemetery in Hatfield. The headstone was five feet tall with an angel on it. We had it inscribed with the standard things: her name, date of birth, and the day she died. At the bottom, a scripture:

"But Jesus said, 'Let the little children come to Me, and do not forbid them; for of such is the kingdom of heaven.'" — Matthew 19:14

At the top, one word in large letters: "SMILE." Andi always signed her name with the word "smile" on all her school papers, with a happy face scrawled beneath.

I decided to drive back to Hatfield to see it. I had not been back since she had been buried. I felt very nervous about this. When I arrived in the adjacent town of Mena, I found a flower shop and stopped in. I wanted a single pink or white rose and a smiley face balloon. They had both. I bought them. Noticing the serious look on my face, the lady behind the counter asked if I was okay. I told her I was not, that I was visiting my daughter's grave for the first time since she was murdered.

"Oh, you're that little girl's mama," she said.

"Yes, her name is Andi."

She nodded and patted my hand. "You take care, okay honey?"

I nodded and left the store with the rose and balloon.

"You take care, okay honey?"

Her words kept playing over and over in my head like a broken record. I didn't even know what "take care" meant. Was it more than just surviving? Breathing? Bathing? Waking up every day?

It was dusk when I pulled into Six-Mile Cemetery in Hatfield. No one else was there, and when I stepped out of the car, it was very quiet and peaceful. In front of me was the huge headstone, located on a slight hill, and the view across the valley was spectacular. It was truly stunning, rising above all the other headstones. It screamed, remember me, in its enormity. I supposed that's what I intended when I picked it out. The birds chirped in the distance, and the gentle wisp of the southern wind whipped my hair. The headstone did indeed make a statement; it said I was precious, larger than life, and it was wrong that I was here. Remember me, don't forget.

It was disturbing to read my daughter's name on it. I put my hand on the side, and it was rough granite. I ran my hand over the front and put my fingers in the etching of the word smile and traced it. Then I walked to the front, knelt, and placed the rose on the slight edge. I noticed a folded note. I picked it up and opened it.

"I didn't know you, but I saw your smile."

I smiled a little, put the note back down, and sat on the damp grass in front of the large stone, knees up. I felt the slight moisture soak the butt of my jeans, but I didn't move. I couldn't. I was paralyzed with the realization that this was true. I thought of Andi's face, her first birthday. How she had not stuck both hands in her cake like most babies but had put a single finger down into the frosting, turned her pink-frosted finger toward my mouth, and said, "Mama, wanna bite?"

I opened my mouth, and she stuck her finger in my mouth.

"Ummm, that's good, Andi," I said.

She giggled, and I lit the candle. We all sang "Happy Birthday," and then I helped her blow out the single green and white candle. The flame lay over and disappeared; the smoke circled up. We all cheered for her. She clapped her baby hands, those tiny, beautiful hands, and giggled.

Let the little children come to me.

A hawk cried out as it flew overhead. The tears began to flow. It was unfathomable that I would never see her again in this lifetime. Anyone passing by might have thought I looked ridiculous, sitting in front of a grave in the grass, gripping a smiley face balloon. I realized I might never be normal again.

After a while, I stood up and noticed the sun had disappeared below the horizon, and darkness was settling in. Looking around for something to tie the balloon to, I found a porcelain angel, slightly heavy, and tied the string in a knot, letting the balloon float up until it reached the end of the string. I stared at it as it swayed gently in the breeze.

Dusting off my jeans, I stepped back to take in the entirety of the grave plot—the headstone, the etched words, her name, the flowers, the lone balloon. The bigger picture hit me hard: this was more than just a grave. It was a murder, a looming capital murder trial, the struggle to breathe, to make sense of this tragedy, to live through what she couldn't, and the endless search for answers. The biggest question remained—why? Would I ever know?

I got into my car with that question echoing in my head. Why? Why? Why? As I pulled away, I glanced in the rearview mirror. The yellow mylar balloon, with its dopey smile, waved goodbye. I didn't want to leave her there in the ground. Even though I knew it was impossible, I still hoped this was all just a nightmare from which I would wake.

PRETRIAL
OCTOBER 1999

We arrived at the courthouse at precisely 9:00 AM and walked up the stairs to the courtroom. When we approached the top, we made a right turn and were stopped by sheriff's deputies who informed us that we had to go through a metal detector due to the death threats hurled at Roberts. I heard some ruckus further down the hall and looked up to see deputies surrounding him as they brought him into a side door of the courtroom. He was wearing a bulletproof vest; his hands were cuffed in front of him. Feeling frustrated that law enforcement had decided to protect a person they were trying to send to death row, I emptied my pockets and purse, feeling very annoyed. I stepped through a large metal detector on loan to the county courtesy of the FBI. The machine didn't beep when I walked through because, unlike the killer who had been brought to a separate door, protected by a bulletproof vest, I was not a cold-blooded baby killer. He was! It all felt backward.

We took our seats as the deputies brought Karl in. He stared at the floor, never once making eye contact. Coward.

"All rise; court is now in session," the sheriff stated loudly, his voice echoing through the room.

The judge entered and said, "You may be seated."

The defense team pleaded for motion after motion concerning the cruelty of the death penalty, and the judge denied most of their requests. He did, however, grant Karl the motion to wear civilian clothing to his court proceedings, but that was it. The entire session lasted only minutes and felt very formal. It was just dry paperwork; no mention of the person Andi was or the devastation we all felt. But we were all there, filling the courtroom, all of us who loved her, her family, to see the beginnings of justice for her. To put the monster who strangled her where he belonged—death row—to face execution and meet his fate. To pay his debt to society. This was the beginning of a very long process we were all aware of. I didn't know about everyone else, but I was in for the long haul. I would see justice served.

The judge set the trial for February 14, 2000.

Happy Valentine's Day.

CHAPTER 13
TEAM HOPE, WASHINGTON DC
NOVEMBER, 1999

Slain girl's mother to stand for daughter

▶ She says the carefree 12-year-old wouldn't want her "to curl up and wither away."

By Linda Martin

She was always drawing roses or writing the word "smile" on everything, including a homework assignment that was marked with an "F," said Rebecca DeMauro, who chuckled as she remembered her happy, carefree 12-year-old daughter, Andrea Nicole Brewer.

The light moment was a brief break from the crushing reality that on Saturday DeMauro will attend her daughter's funeral in Mena, Ark.

The word smile will be engraved on the front of Andrea Nicole Brewer's tombstone, her mother said. "Andi," as she was affectionately called by those who knew her, will be engraved on the back.

Weather permitting, pink and white balloons will be released during Saturday's service to symbolize youth and innocence.

"I want everybody to know she was just a little girl who didn't deserve this," DeMauro said.

Andi, who attended second and third grades at Barnes Elementary School in Owasso, was raped and strangled May 15. Her uncle, Karl Douglas Roberts, 31, of Cove, Ark., is accused in the slaying, authorities said. Roberts is the brother-in-law of Andi's father, Greg Brewer, 31, of Hatfield, Ark.

She had been living with her father for the past 18 months, said DeMauro, who lives in Skiatook with her husband, Kristofer DeMauro, 30, a captain with the Owasso Fire Department.

When DeMauro received the news about her daughter, "I lost my mind. I totally flipped," she said.

Now on Friday, speaking from the funeral home in Mena, she is trying to manage life minute by minute, she said. To do more is unmanageable right now, she said.

"Everybody keeps telling me that I'm going to be mad at God," but she's not.

"I know God didn't do this. I know it's Satan that has done this. I know if I turn against God, I don't have anything to lean on."

She has two choices, DeMauro said.

"I can either go into a corner, curl up and die, or I can stand up and fight. I've chosen to stand up and fight for my little girl. She wouldn't want me to curl up and wither away.

"I just want any kind of justice I can get. I don't want her to be forgotten."

DeMauro said she and Brewer divorced in 1992. Since then they both remarried but maintained good relations for the welfare of their two daughters, Andi and Melani, 10, she said.

Andi, who was very close to her father, wanted to live with him to be around her new baby brother, DeMauro said.

"She was very adamant about it."

She told her mother that if she could live with her father, she would "be good and do good work in school," so DeMauro finally agreed, she said. Andi spent summers and holidays with her mother.

The last time DeMauro saw her daughter was spring break in April, when they went on a shopping spree for Andi's birthday, she said. She last talked with her daughter on Mother's Day.

She described Andi as a "beautiful person. She had a heart of gold."

She was a "very popular" child who played basketball, loved the outdoors, fishing, horses and riding four-wheelers.

According to her teachers in Owasso, she was "very talkative."

"She got a lot of demerits for talking," DeMauro said.

But "she was a good little Christian girl," DeMauro said. She wanted to be a Christian singer when she grew up, like her favorites, Crystal Lewis and dc talk. She took everywhere the compact disc player her mother gave her for Christmas, DeMauro said.

DeMauro said she visited her daughter's classroom and asked to see the desk on which Andi had carved her initials — for which she'd received a demerit.

Andi's teacher showed DeMauro the desk but said Andi had since been moved to another desk. DeMauro asked to see the reassigned desk.

There on the reassigned desk was another carving of Andi's name.

"She had sneaked in and engraved her name again."

A benefit fund has been set up in Andrea Brewer's name at the Union Bank, Mena, AR 71953. The account number is 407763.

Linda Martin can be reached at 581-8381.

Colleen Nick called to ask if I had ever considered volunteer work. I had been searching for something to help me cope, and I was willing to try anything to lift the fog that left too much time for me to think and get angry. She informed me that a grant from the U.S.

Department of Justice had funded the creation of Team HOPE, a parent support group for families of missing children. She thought I would be great at helping others through this organization. Was I interested?

I thought it over and decided that perhaps it would be a good idea to channel the pain. I called Colleen back and told her I was in. The training would be held in November. It had only been six months since Andi had been killed, but I needed this—for me, for my sanity.

The American Eagle plane left the ground and leveled out. I closed my eyes and said a silent prayer. I felt exhausted but relieved to be alone with my thoughts, to sort out what had happened at the pretrial. The flight would take me to Dallas-Fort Worth and then connect me to Reagan International Airport in Washington, DC. I was bound for the National Center for Missing and Exploited Children to be trained for Team HOPE (Help Offering Parents Empowerment). After the training, I would be connected to families whose cases were similar to Andi's to help guide them through their pain. Part of me thought it was too soon to embark on such an endeavor, but another part realized I needed something to help channel the pain. I needed like-minded people in my life.

The flight attendant asked if I would like a drink. I thought about asking for a strong one, but because I still halfway cared about what church people thought of me, I opted for a ginger ale. She set it down in front of me, and I took a drink, letting the cool liquid slip down my throat. The roar of the plane engine was comforting, and I felt some of the tension begin to release. Before long, I was asleep. No nightmares came, and for that, I was thankful.

After a layover in Dallas-Fort Worth, I boarded a different airliner and headed for the Nation's Capitol. After a while, the man next to me tapped me on the shoulder and told me we were over DC. I looked out the window, and the first thing I saw was the Washington Monument. I was in awe. It made me feel so small and a little bit scared; I was just a girl from Kansas. The realization that my sole purpose was to be trained to help other parents who would go through what I was now living struck me deeply. I felt sorry for those I would meet in the future because right then, they were at home with their living child, not realizing that their world would one day be shattered. I wished I knew who they were so I could tell them to hold their child tight and never let go. No one ever believes that tragedy can happen to them until it does. I certainly never thought in a million years that I would be the parent of a child who had been abducted and murdered.

After the plane landed and I deplaned, I walked up the jet bridge and stepped into the terminal. I stopped, my breath catching in my throat. People rushed to and fro, scattering to their destinations, but I couldn't move. Everything was so big, and I felt so small. I had never seen such a busy place and didn't know what to do. I dug in my purse for the itinerary and learned I needed to take a cab to the Alexandrian Hotel in Alexandria, Virginia, where a room had been reserved in my name. I walked through the terminal feeling numb and tried to act as though I knew what I was doing; I had no clue. Finally, I saw a sign that said "Taxi." I tried my best to hail a cab and succeeded. I piled in and told the driver where to take me.

I spent the night in the most beautiful hotel I had ever been to. The next morning, I walked around the block to the National Center for Missing and Exploited Children located in the Charles B. Wang building. The operation was state of the art. The Team HOPE project director greeted me and pointed me to my place at the table in the Jimmy Ryce Law Enforcement Training Center. A placard with my name marked the spot where I was supposed to sit. I was early, and the training room was empty. So, I took some time to gaze around the walls. I noticed photos of missing children—many of them. I started to realize that I was not alone. These walls were full of heartache. In front of each seat, I recognized the names of people from very high-profile abduction cases.

Vicki Kelly, mother of Tommy, who had been abducted and murdered. Patty Wetterling, mother of Jacob, age 11, who had been abducted at gunpoint eleven years ago and was still missing. Don and Claudine Ryce, parents of Jimmy, age 9, who was abducted, raped, and murdered in Florida. The training center where I stood was named in his honor. My friend, Colleen, was there representing The Morgan Nick Foundation. Marc Klaas, father of Polly, who had written to me in May, was also there.

I sat down and flipped through the literature placed before me. Then, someone tapped me on the shoulder. I turned around, and Marc Klaas extended his hand.

"Rebecca? Marc Klaas."

When our eyes met, I wanted to bawl, to have a huge crying episode and sit with him, asking him to tell me exactly what was going to happen to me. I wanted to know how he had survived this horror for five years and still managed to introduce himself to people without breaking down. I wanted to know it all. But I smiled, knowing we shared the same pain. His pain was my pain. It was common ground, and it was ugly. I took his hand and shook it.

"It is an honor to meet you, Mr. Klaas," I replied.

"I am so sorry about your daughter, Andi. And please, call me Marc."

"I'm sorry about Polly."

A friend once told me that there is a difference between sympathy and empathy. Everyone can have sympathy, but only those who have experienced what you have can feel empathy. Marc was the first person I had met who truly empathized with me. I felt honored and relieved to meet him face-to-face. I hoped he could help me make sense of this mess.

The first night after the training session, we all met for dinner. We talked for hours about our children. We reminisced and cried, but most of all, we were there for each other. Finally, I was in the company of people who understood me. I didn't have to worry about them being uncomfortable around me or changing the subject. They listened to what I said about Andi, and I listened as they spoke about their children. After dinner, we decided to go to Murphy's Pub, a wonderful Irish bar in Alexandria. We laughed and sang old Irish songs. I felt alive. It was the first time I smiled. Vicki sat down next to Marc and told me to lean in so we could take a picture. We both leaned toward Marc, and for the first time in months, a smile spread across my face. And it was captured. A twinge of guilt touched me for a minute, but then I realized I was among my people—the ones who wouldn't judge. And it felt good. I almost felt normal.

Almost.

When the training ended, we stood in a circle holding hands, each of us saying a few words. When my turn came, I spoke from the heart: "I never asked or wished to be part of this club that no one wants to join, but now that I'm here, I'm grateful to be with all of you."

Everyone cried and smiled. Then we all hugged. I had made friends for life. It was a step in the right direction. My path to advocacy had begun.

CHAPTER 14
THE BATTLE IS WON,
BUT THE WAR IS NOT OVER
HOLIDAYS 1999

Thanksgiving 1998 had been wonderful. We spent it with my family in Topeka, Kansas, hosted by my Uncle Denny and Aunt Barbara Petty. They lived in a beautiful home set in the center of a million trees overlooking a valley below. The main wall in the living room was a glass front that pointed toward the forest. A beautiful deck circled the home, and at any given time, you could see the squirrels running back and forth on the railing. My uncle talked about trying to figure out a way to keep the squirrels from chewing up his deck. Then he fried a turkey while we all helped prepare the fixings. My aunt Barb filled water balloons for the kids to throw at each other on that unseasonably warm fall day. Finally, we sat down to dinner, gave thanks, and ate until we were stuffed. Laughter and love were etched in my brain to this very day. After the huge meal, the entire

Petty clan went on a nature hike. We walked for a mile or so, enjoying the scenery and our family. Andi was as happy as I had ever seen her. I remember thinking that it wouldn't be long before she would start driving and dating.

This was my last Thanksgiving with her.

Thanksgiving of 1999 was nothing like that. We spent it with Mom and my stepdad, where the world just seemed gray, and the turkey seemed dry, although I was sure it wasn't. But everyone sat in awkwardness, making small talk. Mom brought up something that Andi had said or done, and we all slightly smiled through our grief in remembrance. Then my stepdad burst into tears, pushed back from the table, and rushed out the back door. I made eye contact with Mom and stood up to go find him and hug him or do something for him. With tears in her eyes, she shook her head and said, "Just let him go. He's been doing that a lot; he can't talk about Andi without breaking down like that."

Thanksgiving felt like a big lie that year. We all tried to pretend, but when my stepfather left the table, the truth was told in his single action. That's what we all wanted to do. Run.

Kris, the girls, and I didn't stay long. We finished picking at our food and decided to go home. On our way out the door, I hugged my mom extra tight, told her I loved her, and asked her to tell Dad I loved him, too. He hadn't returned from wherever he had run to. She said she would and assured me that he would be okay.

After Thanksgiving, Kris pulled the Christmas tree out of the attic. I was about as excited for Christmas as I had been for Thanksgiving. I siphoned through the ornaments and found all of Andi's. Little handprint wreaths, reindeer, and golden ornaments with her name and date etched for every year she had been alive. After Christmas each year, I would take the girls, rummage through the clearance department for ornaments, and for about a quarter, they would find an ornament they liked, and we would have their name engraved on it. I placed Andi's eleven ornaments in front of me and lost it. AGAIN.

I didn't want to celebrate Christmas.

Kris set up the tree and strung the lights. The kids wanted to hang the ornaments on the tree, so I let them do the honors. Melanie asked if she could hang Andi's. In my mind, I had assumed that we wouldn't put her things on the tree that year, that I would wrap them up in a box and just start fresh. I did not understand why I felt this way. I just assumed it would be easier, but then I came to my senses. I picked up the eleven ornaments, handed them to Melanie, and she handed her sister a few. They both smiled and hung them up. Melanie hung hers a little higher, and Kristin went low. I watched them. I didn't move, just sat there. They still loved Christmas; they were just little girls. They still wanted presents, they still wanted to watch the lights, they still believed in Santa. They still believed.

Believe.

Did I?

Right then, I did not. I believed in nothing, but I went through the motions for them.

Only for them.

That night, I tucked Melanie and Kristin into bed. I sat on the couch, curled my legs underneath me, and watched the Christmas tree lights flicker in unison. I took a sip of chamomile tea and thought about everything that we had been through the past year. All the dreams that had been stolen from us. The things that would never be replaced. How could Christmas ever be the same? How could anything ever be the same? Would I wake up every day for the rest of my life and struggle to get out of bed?

I thought about Andi's first Christmas. She was just beginning to walk. She would hold her arms straight out and take each step cautiously, then fall into my arms. Every move she made, ripping into her packages, every smile was caught on camera. Then I thought about Christmas a few years after that when my sister held a job at JCPenney as a photographer and took Christmas pictures of the girls. How beautiful they were, and how that image is forever frozen in time.

This kind of thing, old snapshots, made me wonder what the purpose of life was, why we were all here. Why had Andi only been given 12 years? What would her legacy be? Would she have one? Should I be her voice? I could barely talk about her without crying.

The lights on the tree kept flickering; they blurred. I hated those tears. I angrily wiped them away and tried hard to feel the Christmas spirit. It wasn't there. I doubted it ever would be again.

Next up was the capital murder trial.

FEBRUARY 2000

• • TUESDAY, FEBRUARY 15, 2000
Copyright © 2000, Arkansas Democrat-Gazette, Inc.

Family wrenched by tragedy again waits for justice

New evidence delays trial of uncle charged in rape, death of 12-year-old

BY CATHY FRYE
ARKANSAS DEMOCRAT-GAZETTE

MENA — Last July, Ann Brewer went to the secluded clearing where her 12-year-old granddaughter, Andi, had been raped and strangled just a few months earlier.

"I thought maybe I could find something of hers," she explains, her voice cracking. "I just wanted to find something."

As she roamed the crime scene, searching vainly for anything that might have belonged to Andi, Brewer fell into a hole, badly injuring her knees and feet. They still hurt, she says.

So does her heart.

Her granddaughter, Andria Nichole Brewer, is dead. And the man accused of the killing was her uncle, a revelation that has left the family shattered.

Karl Roberts, 31, is charged with capital murder and faces the death penalty if he's convicted.

His trial was supposed to begin today.

But much to the disappointment of Andi's many relatives, it was postponed Monday.

New evidence offered recently by the defense prompted prosecutors to file a motion Friday asking for an 11th-hour continuance. Judge Gayle Ford of the 18th Circuit Court West granted the request at a hearing Monday morning in Mena.

A second trial date will be set

Karl Roberts   Andria Brewer

within a few days.

The new evidence includes medical and forensic information regarding an old head injury of Roberts', which is expected to be a key portion of his defense.

"They just now themselves got it," Prosecuting Attorney Tim Williamson said of the defense team. It's been only nine months since the girl's death, he said, adding, "This has been a rather fast setting. We just need more time to look at it."

Defense attorney Darrel Blount fought the delay, saying the prosecution knew about this new information at the beginning of January.

"We say that we advised the state of it, but the state disputes that," Blount said. He wouldn't elaborate on what type of new evidence was found, only confirming that it does have something to do with Roberts' head injury, which occurred 20 years ago when he was hit by a dump truck while riding

See **FAMILY**, Page 6B

Prosecutor Williamson called me two days before Karl's trial was set to begin and informed me that he would ask for a continuance.

"Why?" I asked. I had mentally and emotionally prepared myself.

"Well, ma'am, I am sitting in my office looking at an MRI of Karl's head, and there's a big hole where his brain should be. An old injury to the frontal lobe."

I sat down and took a deep breath.

Robert's defense team would now claim a mental defect.

"The defense is going to try to claim that a mental defect caused Karl to kill Andi. It seems that Karl was hit by a dump truck while riding his bicycle when he was twelve. They have found a doctor from Little Rock who will testify on their behalf. He will say that the type of injury Karl received when he was twelve caused him to snap and have a violent episode," he said. "I'll find a competent physician to dispute this. It's purely a defense tactic. They know Karl doesn't have much of a case. His written confession is his own noose. The defense is trying to buy him life without parole. They are trying everything they know to do to save this guy's life. I don't want you to worry about anything; everything will be okay. I promise."

"Are you sure?"

"Yes, I'm positive. The continuance should buy us enough time to locate a doctor who is well-respected and will say that Karl is competent. And he is. Anyone who can play the drums like he can and hold down a $55,000-a-year job is competent."

To add insult to injury, the next week, I received a letter from the Arkansas Attorney General's office stating that the state victim reparations fund would not be paying for the counseling I had been receiving. When Andi was killed, we were encouraged by the prosecutor's office to get counseling and told the state would pay for it. A psychologist who came to our church (even though I was hit-and-miss attending services at this point) was counseling me weekly. Since he was from Oklahoma, the state of Arkansas refused this request after I had been receiving counseling for about a month. They gave us the option to appeal the decision, and I decided that if things were ever going to change for future victims in Arkansas, then I would do so aggressively.

They set the appeal date for March.

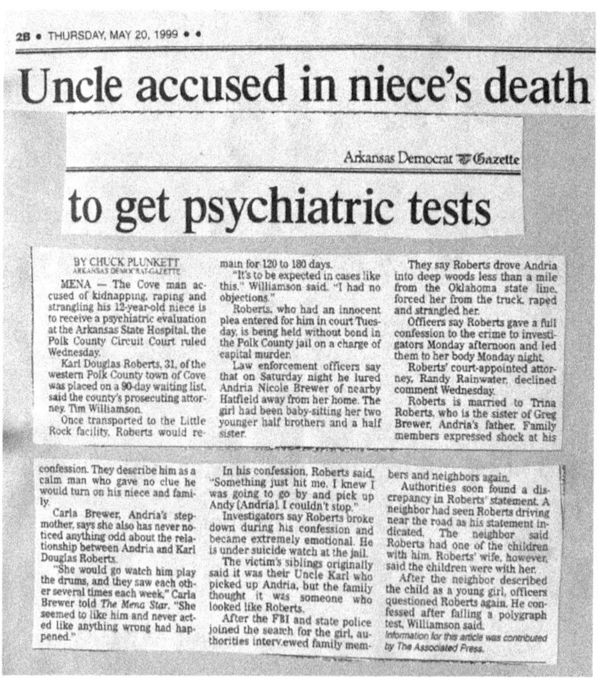

Uncle accused in niece's death

Arkansas Democrat Gazette

to get psychiatric tests

BY CHUCK PLUNKETT
ARKANSAS DEMOCRAT-GAZETTE

MENA — The Cove man accused of kidnapping, raping and strangling his 12-year-old niece is to receive a psychiatric evaluation at the Arkansas State Hospital, the Polk County Circuit Court ruled Wednesday.

Karl Douglas Roberts, 31, of the western Polk County town of Cove was placed on a 90-day waiting list, said the county's prosecuting attorney, Tim Williamson.

Once transported to the Little Rock facility, Roberts would remain for 120 to 180 days.

"It's to be expected in cases like this," Williamson said. "I had no objections."

Roberts, who had an innocent plea entered for him in court Tuesday, is being held without bond in the Polk County jail on a charge of capital murder.

Law enforcement officers say that on Saturday night he lured Andria Nicole Brewer of nearby Hatfield away from her home. The girl had been baby-sitting her two younger half brothers and a half sister.

They say Roberts drove Andria into deep woods less than a mile from the Oklahoma state line, forced her from the truck, raped and strangled her.

Officers say Roberts gave a full confession to the crime to investigators Monday afternoon and led them to her body Monday night.

Roberts' court-appointed attorney, Randy Rainwater, declined comment Wednesday.

Roberts is married to Trina Roberts, who is the sister of Greg Brewer, Andria's father. Family members expressed shock at his confession. They describe him as a calm man who gave no clue he would turn on his niece and family.

Carla Brewer, Andria's stepmother, says she also has never noticed anything odd about the relationship between Andria and Karl Douglas Roberts.

"She would go watch him play the drums, and they saw each other several times each week," Carla Brewer told The Mena Star. "She seemed to like him and never acted like anything wrong had happened."

In his confession, Roberts said, "Something just hit me. I knew I was going to go by and pick up Andy [Andria]. I couldn't stop."

Investigators say Roberts broke down during his confession and became extremely emotional. He is under suicide watch at the jail.

The victim's siblings originally said it was their Uncle Karl who picked up Andria, but the family thought it was someone who looked like Roberts.

After the FBI and state police joined the search for the girl, authorities interviewed family members and neighbors again.

Authorities soon found a discrepancy in Roberts' statement. A neighbor had seen Roberts driving near the road as his statement indicated. The neighbor said Roberts had one of the children with him. Roberts' wife, however, said the children were with her.

After the neighbor described the child as a young girl, officers questioned Roberts again. He confessed after failing a polygraph test, Williamson said.

Information for this article was contributed by The Associated Press.

When March rolled around, I was tired of fighting. It appeared I was in a never-ending battle, fighting to keep Karl from becoming the victim, fighting the state for a few hundred dollars when they had already spent thousands to house, clothe, and feed that confessed child killer, and fighting to keep my sanity. I wanted to give up and let the state keep my money, but Colleen Nick, to my rescue again, encouraged me to fight. She told me the battle was almost won, and victory was right around the corner.

The victim witness coordinator also encouraged me to fight. She volunteered to make the trip to Little Rock with me to attend the hearing. She told me that I would have to stand before the board of directors and tell them why I was appealing. I was terrified.

We made the trip to Little Rock the day before the scheduled hearing. We drove through torrential rain. The roads were slick and wet. I wondered if someone above was trying to tell me to keep fighting or if the devil was beating me up again.

The next morning in the Attorney General's office, I was introduced to some of the staff and told I would be the third hearing on the docket that day. Finally, I was called into a small room. The table and chairs were arranged in the shape of a "U," and I sat in the center, facing the board members. I felt a spotlight shining down on me; there were several others in the room, seated in chairs behind me. I felt so vulnerable. The room was full of people and stuffy. I was sworn in and the hearing began. My heart pounded with full force when one of the board members began reading about our case. She stated that I had been refused reimbursement for counseling services. Then she continued, "On May 15, 1999, 12-year-old

Andria Brewer was abducted from her father's home in Hatfield, Arkansas. She was taken to a remote location where she was raped and strangled."

A few of the board members began to cry.

"Would you like to add anything further before we make the decision about your claim?"

"Yes, I feel like the state of Arkansas is re-victimizing me and my family," I said, no longer able to stop the flow of tears. "We were encouraged to receive counseling..." My voice cracked, and tears dropped from my eyes. I stopped, wiped my face, and took a deep breath.

"My daughter, Andi, was just a little girl. She didn't deserve the things that happened to her," and I couldn't go on. Half the room was crying.

One of the board members, a man with a full beard, spoke up, "I make a motion to pay this family their money. Another thing, do we have to keep this rule about the counselor being licensed within the state of Arkansas only? That is a dumb rule. She doesn't live here, and it would be difficult for her family to drive clear over here once a week for counseling. I make another motion to throw it out."

Both motions were approved. And Andi's story, my story, paved the way for future victims to be able to have the counselor of their choice. I was so happy, not that I got my money back, but that

I had taken a stand about something I believed in. That I had fought "city hall," and won.

I called Colleen and told her the news.

She was ecstatic, "See? You won the battle. Aren't you glad you listened to me and fought?" she said.

"Yes, I am."

"Andi's legacy is living on through you. You should be proud," she said.

I really was. And I knew the small battle was won, but I was also aware that the war was not over.

CHAPTER 15
JURY SELECTION
A VERY BAD MAN, INDEED
MAY 2000

Jury selection was set to begin on May 8, 2000. I was scared because Kris had decided it was best to stay home with the girls and not attend until the jury was selected and the actual trial was underway.

I did not want to be alone. I was upset by his choice, but he didn't budge. I was not in the mood to fight his decision, and I had no choice but to just do this part alone. He said he needed things to be normal for the girls, and though I somewhat agreed, those poor girls hadn't had a day of normalcy since this whole damn thing happened.

Melanie had been bullied at school for having a "dead sister," and I had to go pick her up because she was crying so hard she was inconsolable. After we left, her teacher stepped up and gave the bullies the chewing they deserved.

Kristin was deathly afraid of strangers; the elderly man who worked as a door greeter at Wal-Mart tried to give her a sucker, and she refused. When he handed it to her despite her refusal, she threw it at him. It bounced off his chest, and she screamed, "I don't want it," and ran to wrap herself around my waist. The man looked perplexed, and I just said, "Long story." There was no parenting manual for these situations. I tried to do my best.

I left for Mena on Sunday evening, May 7th. My heart flipped and flopped the entire drive. I wished I had visited my doctor for a prescription for Xanax to help me calm down. I did not know what to expect attending jury selection, much less a murder trial, but, alas, there I was. The prosecutor had told me it was going to be individual voir dire; I had to look up what that even meant. Apparently, the court was going to interview each potential juror individually to make sure, by their own testimony, that they could be fair and impartial.

We had already dealt with a local church petitioning to have the trial moved to another county, but the judge denied the change of venue. I believed in having a jury of peers rightfully judge the accused after hearing evidence in a case, so I was thankful for the judge's decision. I didn't think a local church should meddle in court proceedings of an admitted child murderer. I had heard rumors of a few preachers in town wanting to go into the jail to meet and pray with Uncle Karl. These same preachers never reached out to my family once. I felt very bitter about this. I guessed they all assumed I would reach the pearly gates, even with hate, rage, and unforgiveness in my heart. I found it disgusting.

The next morning, when I arrived at the Polk County courthouse, I heard a commotion in the breezeway connecting the main building to the jail. I glanced up to see two rows of heavily armed police officers creating a barrier around Karl Roberts. It was the first time I had seen him in a year. His appearance was that of a man who had not been outside in a long while. His skin was pasty and white; he looked a lot older. His hands hung in front of his body in handcuffs. A bulletproof vest covered his torso.

Prosecutor Williamson knew the bulletproof vest annoyed me. He saw the discontent in my face and knew what I was going to say. He answered before I could ask.

"He's had a whole lot of death threats again."

I didn't say anything; just rolled my eyes.

But, of course, by all means, let's keep a child killer alive so we can execute him later. Makes sense.

The sarcasm, I felt, was almost palpable.

Williamson put his hand on the small of my back and guided me in. The courtroom filled up with family members, friends, onlookers, and a few reporters. It was a full house for only a jury selection. The proceedings began at 9:00 AM sharp.

The prospective jurors were brought into the courtroom from all walks of life—young, old, rich, poor. The judge informed them that jury selection would be based on *voir dire*. Each potential juror was brought in and questioned. Thus began the day. One after another, each juror was questioned extensively. When the potential jurors were allowed to speak, it didn't sound good for Karl Roberts. Hearing that most of his peers wanted him to be hung on the courthouse lawn must have been difficult. In my mind, he deserved to hear it. He was this community's boogeyman. He was the one who caused them all to lock their doors, sleep with guns on their nightstands, and force their children to play inside. He was truly a very bad man. Most people brought in for questioning had no sympathy for him. They seemed disgusted by being in the same room.

Karl listened, head down, barely moving except to occasionally pick up a pencil and pretend to take notes. I studied every move he made. I imagined the screams he had likely heard from my daughter, yet he still sat calmly. His hands bothered me the most. I had thought about his hands a lot—those hands that had gently held his toddler son while watching me beg and plead in front of the camera for my daughter's return. Those hands that had played the drums on the afternoon of May 15, 1999, were the same hands that put themselves around my daughter's throat that evening and squeezed the life from her. I looked up at his hands again as he laid the pencil down, crossed them one on top of the other, and kept looking down at the table.

A very bad man, indeed.

For the next week, people were paraded in and out of the courtroom and questioned about everything from their family life to their job, to whether they had kids or grandkids, to their belief on the death penalty.

"He's a baby killer, and he deserves the death penalty."

"He ain't innocent, he took them to her body."

"There's a tree out to the side of this courthouse, I got a rope in my pickup."

"To be honest, I do not know why we are wasting tax dollars on this SOB."

But there were also those who said, they could be fair and impartial.

"I can listen to the evidence and make up my mind for proper punishment."

"I'm not God. I wouldn't feel comfortable passing down a sentence of death. I mean, I could probably give life without parole if he was guilty, but never death. It's just my religious belief."

"I went to school with Greg and Becki. Greg is two years older than me, and I graduated with Becki."

"I worked with the little girl's step-granddad building a chicken house one time in Cove, out the same road where that piece of shit," points to Karl, "took that little girl and raped her. He needs to fry. We need to bring Old Sparky back for this case."

I never thought a jury would be chosen. I wanted to tell those who kept saying they needed to execute him on the spot to just be quiet and say they would be willing to listen and make a judgment.

Just shut up! Shut up and get on this jury. Then you can vote to execute him. I am so ready for justice.

It took every bit of a week and all of my energy and patience, but finally, twelve jurors were chosen along with three alternates. By the end of it all, I was exhausted. I followed my mother out of the courtroom and pulled out a pack of my now beloved Swisher Sweets. There was a designated "smoke hole" for us heathens (that's what the church folk would say) who smoke. It was all new to me because I had never smoked prior to this turn of events in my life. Nerves. My mom was there with me and bums a smoke. Nerves for her, too, I guess.

"You need a light? I'd say so after that shitshow going on in there," a man chuckled behind me and patted me twice on the back.

I turned around, and it was Karl's defense attorney, Daryl Blount. He had his lighter lit with his hand cupped around it, holding it toward me. My eyes turned stone cold, and I looked him in the face. Swisher still between my fingers hanging at my side.

I leaned in. I spoke in a calm manner. "I am not your friend; do not speak to me as such. You are defending a baby killer in there. And a word of advice, stay the fuck away from me and my family. Understand?"

His eyes widened, and he opened his mouth to respond, but then he closed it, and his caterpillar mustache hung over his lip. He closed the lid to the Zippo, snuffed out the flame, and stepped back.

"No offense, ma'am. Just trying to be polite."

"Capital murder and politeness don't exactly go hand in hand. Ever consider that?" I took my mother by the arm, and we went around to the front of the courthouse. We never went back to the smoke hole again.

"Sorry, I cursed, momma. I know you hate the 'F' word."

"Screw that bastard," she said.

It had taken six days to pick the eight-man, four-woman jury. Three alternates were chosen as well, the last two on May 12, 2000. This meant the capital murder trial would begin Monday, May 15. Kristin's 5th birthday.

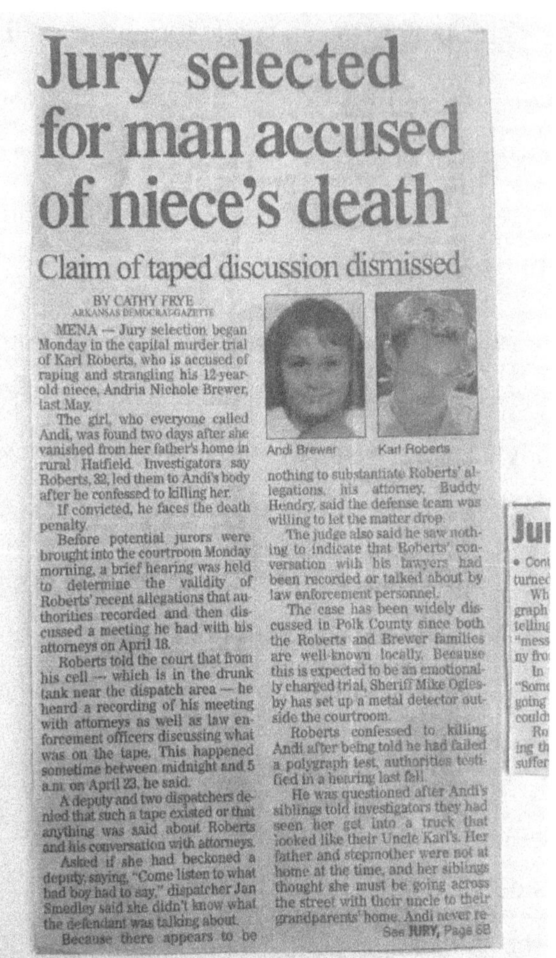

Jury selected for man accused of niece's death

Claim of taped discussion dismissed

BY CATHY FRYE
ARKANSAS DEMOCRAT-GAZETTE

MENA — Jury selection began Monday in the capital murder trial of Karl Roberts, who is accused of raping and strangling his 12-year-old niece, Andria Nichole Brewer, last May.

The girl, who everyone called Andi, was found two days after she vanished from her father's home in rural Hatfield. Investigators say Roberts, 32, led them to Andi's body after he confessed to killing her.

If convicted, he faces the death penalty.

Before potential jurors were brought into the courtroom Monday morning, a brief hearing was held to determine the validity of Roberts' recent allegations that authorities recorded and then discussed a meeting he had with his attorneys on April 18.

Roberts told the court that from his cell — which is in the drunk tank near the dispatch area — he heard a recording of his meeting with attorneys as well as law enforcement officers discussing what was on the tape. This happened sometime between midnight and 5 a.m. on April 23, he said.

A deputy and two dispatchers denied that such a tape existed or that anything was said about Roberts and his conversation with attorneys.

Asked if she had beckoned a deputy, saying, "Come listen to what bad boy had to say," dispatcher Jan Smedley said she didn't know what the defendant was talking about.

Because there appears to be

Andi Brewer   Karl Roberts

nothing to substantiate Roberts' allegations, his attorney, Buddy Hendry, said the defense team was willing to let the matter drop.

The judge also said he saw nothing to indicate that Roberts' conversation with his lawyers had been recorded or talked about by law enforcement personnel.

The case has been widely discussed in Polk County since both the Roberts and Brewer families are well-known locally. Because this is expected to be an emotionally charged trial, Sheriff Mike Oglesby has set up a metal detector outside the courtroom.

Roberts confessed to killing Andi after being told he had failed a polygraph test, authorities testified in a hearing last fall.

He was questioned after Andi's siblings told investigators they had seen her get into a truck that looked like their Uncle Karl's. Her father and stepmother were not at home at the time, and her siblings thought she must be going across the street with their uncle to their grandparents' home. Andi never re-

See JURY, Page 6B

The final night of jury selection, I drove back to Hatfield to put another pink rose and a smiley face balloon on Andi's grave. The headstone seemed to tower above me as I sat on the bench her grandfather had recently placed in front of it. I touched her name on the stone and outlined it with my fingers. I tried to remember the sound of her voice, the sweetness of her giggle. I found it difficult to do that day because all I could hear was the sound of the reverb of that damn courtroom—the booming male voices arguing for this juror or that one. I just wanted to hear Andi's sweet laugh and feel her give me an unexpected "slug bug, no tag backs" punch in the arm. Instead, I felt punched in the gut. Alone again in this solitary resting ground and a headache from hell.

The tears began to stream down my face. Waterworks again. I had to try to get this bawling under control.

"You need a light? I'd say so after that shit show going on in there."

I HATE YOU, GOD!

"You can't say that about God," it was my mother's voice in my head.

I wondered if I would burn in hell for all eternity if I turned my fist toward heaven and told God what I really thought. Realizing He knew what I was thinking anyway, I decided I might as well say it out loud. So, for the first time in my life, I used utter, raw, wretched profanity against the Creator of the Universe. And I stomped, spit, kicked, and sputtered. Then I threw in a few rude gestures to boot. If I was gonna get struck by lightning, by God, I wanted it to be good. And then I beat the shit out of that stupid mylar balloon with the smiley face.

"Stop smiling at me, you wretched fucker."

It was a full Clark Griswold fit, and when I finished, I plopped down on the concrete bench in front of the word "SMILE." I outwardly groaned and rolled my eyes for good measure just to let

God know that I wasn't quite over my dramatic fit.

I do not recall if the wind had been blowing before, but when I was done, I realized a gentle breeze was making its way across the cemetery and gently blew across my face.

I stopped bawling and cursing.

"Stop that, God, can't I just have a minute to throw one fit?"

Everything stopped. The breeze, the crickets, the frogs croaking, everything. It was silent. I stood up and first looked around to make sure no one saw me act crazy, and then I dug a tissue out of my purse and blew my nose. I smoothed out the front of my shirt and shook my hair back. The flat mylar balloon was still grinning on the ground after my massive balloon ass-kicking, so I picked it up, smoothed it out, and laid it on her grave topper. It was not as pretty as it would have been had it been floating gently. But that was the best I could do. I laid the rose on top of it. Then I drove away from the cemetery. I didn't look back this time. I didn't want to see her headstone in the rearview mirror. I just couldn't that day.

I dreaded the next week. The capital murder trial would begin for the man who raped and strangled my Andi.

My Andit Bandit.

STOP BAWLING!!!!

I couldn't.

CHAPTER 16
THE TRIAL
MAY 15, 2000

The trial was set to begin exactly one year to the day, Andi was murdered, Kristin's 5th birthday. The girls stayed behind in Oklahoma with trusted friends. We had spent Saturday afternoon celebrating Kristin's birthday, trying very hard not to remind her how her last birthday had run off the rails. The celebration was nice, but my mind was elsewhere. Not fair to her, I realized. Poor baby.

That evening, I snuggled her in my lap before we left Oklahoma. I realized she had grown a lot this past year. But even though she was five, she still had baby hands, chubby fingers, and pronounced dimples above her fingers. She held my face in her hands and said, "Mommy, why are you so sad all the time now? Is it because Andi went to heaven?"

I pulled her close, embraced her tight, and smelled her hair; she smelled like cookies and dirt. I loved her more at that moment than I had ever loved her. Her concern for me was so childlike yet so mature. I never wanted to let go. I looked to my left, and Melanie was watching. I extended my arm to her.

"Group hug," and she piled in the middle of us. I tickled her ribs, and she squealed loudly, as she always did. I loved them. Nothing was more precious than that. My girls.

DAY ONE
TESTIMONY TAKEN FROM ACTUAL COURT
DOCUMENTS

The Polk County courthouse sat on a square lot in downtown Mena, Arkansas. The courthouse itself was a square, three-story building. Two of the floors were above ground, and the third was a basement. The front of the courthouse faced southeast. Double glass doors gaped open like an ominous mouth. Huge marble slabs flanked the front steps, resembling the paws of a giant creature at rest. The large casement-style windows on the building were eyes looking in all different directions. The throat of the courthouse was a central hallway along which old wooden chairs were placed sporadically.

The first day of the trial began with a thunderstorm that dumped torrential rain. We ducked inside the courthouse out of the storm. Camera crews and reporters from Fort Smith and Little Rock had their satellite trucks parked out front. We learned that they would be doing live feeds during the five and six o'clock news.

The trial would be held in the second-floor courtroom. A large, wide staircase led and then turned 180 degrees, and then up again to the second floor. At the top of the steps, you could turn left, which would take you into a room that served as a waiting area for witnesses. Turning right led you down a dark-paneled hallway with a double wooden door on the left. This door led into the courtroom. When we came up the stairs, the lights from the television camera crews snapped on, blinding us for a moment. They filmed us as we went through the security check and metal detector. Deputies searched my purse for weapons. They searched my entire family like we were criminals; this was disheartening.

"He's had a whole lot of death threats."

The courtroom was filled with deputies and city police officers, eight in total. They were stationed around the room. The only separation on the courtroom floor was a wooden railing about three feet high. It had a swing gate in the middle, like a courtroom in the movies. The reverb in the room was almost deafening. Everyone was talking in hushed tones, but it echoed like crazy.

The jury seats were on the left side of the courtroom. In front of the room was a large wooden structure where the judge would sit. In front of the judge was a long table where the prosecution and defense teams sat.

The room was packed full and stuffy. I spotted Colleen and her mom, Joanna. I approached, hugged, and thanked them for coming to support Andi; then, I proceeded to the front pew. My parents, Rick and Ann, were there, as well as most of the Brewers. Distant cousins, onlookers, and reporters filled the rest of the courtroom. My stepdad, Lloyd, opted out; he was too grief-stricken and still too devastated. The victim witness coordinator sat directly behind me. On the other side of the room were a few supporters of Karl: his parents, his wife (Andi's paternal aunt), and their pastor. The reporters chose to sit on the defendant's side because there was way more room. TV cameras were not allowed in the courtroom.

Judge Ford, an older man with graying hair and a kind face, swept into the courtroom at nine o'clock sharp. His dark-rimmed glasses complimented his black court robe.

"All rise, court will now be in session," Sheriff Oglesby said.

"You may be seated," was the judge's reply. He ordered the clerk to read the jurors the oath. When all jurors and alternates were sworn in, he said, "Be seated, ladies and gentlemen. Before we start, let me show the record that the Defendant and his attorneys are present. Is the state ready for trial?"

"Yes, Your Honor," Williamson replied.

"Is the Defense ready for trial?"

"Yes, Your Honor."

The judge continued, "Ladies and gentlemen, you have been selected and sworn as the jury to try the case of the State of Arkansas versus Karl Douglas Roberts. This is a criminal case. The information for this case has been read to you. It is your solemn responsibility to determine the guilt or innocence of the defendant based solely on the evidence as it is presented to you in this trial. Mr. Williamson, you may make an opening statement on behalf of the State of Arkansas."

A hush fell onto the courtroom.

"Thank you, Your Honor." All eyes were on the prosecutor. I took my first real look at the jury. I did not recognize any of them. They looked like normal, everyday folks. I felt sorry for them. I was not sure if they realized what they were in for. I couldn't imagine living a quiet life and then being chosen to render judgment of something so wrong and evil.

"If it pleases the Court, counsel, ladies and gentlemen of the jury, in *voir dire,* the judge reads to you the charge that the state alleges the defendant has committed. *That* charge is capital murder. The State intends to introduce the evidence to you that one year and one day ago today, this defendant raped and killed his 12-year-old niece, Andria Nichole Brewer."

He paused slightly, making eye contact with the jurors. His blue eyes jump, his mouth set on telling this story of evil that has fallen on this small town.

"Evidence, in this case, is going to be that it was Saturday, May 15, 1999, a pretty typical Saturday around the Roberts' and Brewers' household. Evidence will show that Andria lived with her father, Greg Brewer, north of Hatfield, off a county road just off Highway 71. She had three smaller stepsiblings there in the house where she also lived. Her mother, Rebecca, lives in Tulsa, Oklahoma, because her parents, Greg and Rebecca, are divorced and had joint custody, and Andria was living with her father, Greg, at the time. Greg Brewer's residence is very close to the Charles and Ann Brewer residence. There is probably no more than 400 yards that separate the two. You cannot see one residence from the other because of a jog in the driveway and a densely wooded area."

He continued, "I think you will see in the course of this trial that both the Roberts and Brewer families were close families at the time. You see, Karl Roberts, the defendant in this case, is married to Trina. Trina and Greg are brother and sister. Charles and Ann

Brewer are their parents. Therefore, Charles and Ann Brewer are the grandparents of Andria Brewer. As was common practice on May 15, 1999, the defendant, Karl Roberts, in the late afternoon hours, sometime around 4:00 o'clock, was at the Charles and Ann Brewer residence. He and Charles had built a building where Karl could keep his drum set, and Charles would play along with the music. Sometimes, they would have other people over to play. On that day, as usual, Karl drank about a six-pack of Miller beer in the afternoon. It was hot; the drum set was pulled outside of the building because it was muggy, similar to the weather we have been having, except a little warmer, and he played his drum set all afternoon."

Williamson paced in front of the jury box. The way he carried himself, the way he talked to the jurors in his thick southern drawl, handling them as though they were delicate china, portrayed the essence of a man who intended to win a case he strongly believed in. I hung on every word. I was reliving every second. I could see it as a picture show in my head.

"There was a dinner prepared by Ann and Trina that night. The family ate while Karl continued to play his drums in the front yard. Evidence will show that Karl ate his dinner. I think that you will see that he ate salmon patties and 'taters,' according to him, and he drank some sweet tea. After eating dinner, as was his customary practice about 7:30 at night, he was to have gone to his parents, Bob and Peggy Roberts' house some distance away. Evidence will show that he has been employed by the same company for six years. It will show that he was married to Trina, show that he had two small children, a son and a daughter.

"But something happened on that day...Karl Roberts left the Brewer residence. Told his wife that he was going to his parents. That is what his wife believed, what Ann and Charles believed. That wasn't where he was going. Instead, as soon as he left the Brewer residence, Karl Roberts made an immediate left-hand turn down that county road just out of sight of the Charles Brewer residence, and he got halfway up the driveway and saw that Greg Brewer's truck wasn't there and he knew that Carla Brewer wasn't home because she worked the night shift at the Hatfield Super Stop. She'd get home around 10:00. He continued on down that driveway another 200 yards, got out and knocked on the front door.

"Andria was cooking dinner for her siblings. He told her to hurry up and come with him. She asked why. 'Just get in the truck.' She did. It was her uncle. She thought she'd be right back, and he left with her, went out and turned left out of the driveway and continued on by Bob's Auto, driving out."

The jury hung on to every word, eyes wide. Mesmerized.

"Getting kind of late, it's not dark yet, meets William Padgett, a good friend of the family, on the road. They meet and wave to each other. William sees him and thinks nothing of it. It's quite common for Karl to be leaving at that time of night. William saw a little head up against the far window of Karl's truck, up against the corner, little bitty head sticking up over the dash. William assumed it was Karl's 4-year-old daughter. Nothing happened, and they drove on.

"Uncle Karl decides to take a right and drives out a quarter mile or so to Highway 71 north of Hatfield, takes a left, and drives through Hatfield, continues on to Cove, just like he was going to his parents' house. He gets to Cove, takes a right at Randall's grocery. Goes on a county road and continues to drive west toward Oklahoma. The road takes a sharp left-hand turn after the pavement ends and borders on a clear-cut. Less than a mile from the Oklahoma line he goes straight instead, down an old logging road."

Williamson took a deep breath. My fingernails were gone, chewed to the quick. He continued.

"The sheriff will tell you when you drive down that logging road what it looks like. It starts out as a red clay road, and if you keep driving further, he will tell you he sees a lot of trash lying on the side of that logging road, an old Hungry Hound Restaurant sign, shoes, junk and garbage. If you drive further down this road, there are mud holes that have been filled in and the trees seem to get closer and closer. You continue to drive into this funnel. As you drive further down this road, it gets kind of dark down there. It looks like, from one perspective, it might be the end of the road. That's where Karl parked his truck. Now, on the way, Andi wanted to know what was happening. She wanted to know where they were going. 'Why are you doing this? Take me home!' Further, she was upset, the truck stops, she asks, 'What are you going to do to me?' and he tells her.

I'll let you hear the evidence from what he told her. He pulled her out of the truck, forced her down on the ground, pulled her pants and panties off and raped her. After he raped her, I think the evidence is going to show he says he realized he couldn't take her home then."

Mocking Karl, he continued, '*I mashed my thumbs in her throat, and I squeezed until her face turned blue and she went limp, quit moving, quit fighting.*'

"He says then that he got off her and pulled his pants back up, removed her shirt and bra, drug her off in the woods, covered her with some limbs—old dead wet pine limbs that he found in a clear-cut—covered her body as best he could so it wouldn't be discovered, collected up all her clothing, anything else he could find that belonged to her, put them in his truck, backed out and drove off.

"As soon as Karl got to the Buffalo Creek Bridge, he stopped and threw the shirt, pants, panties and bra in the creek. It had just stormed, and it had been raining. Backed up, he drove less than a half-mile to his parents' house. And that's where he was at 8:41 PM that night when his wife, Trina, called him from Charles and Ann Brewer's house to tell him that Andi was missing. So, see, her stepmom had called about 7:30 that night to make sure everything was okay with the kids. Andi didn't answer the phone. She wasn't supposed to be anywhere else; she was supposed to be looking out after the children. Trina went over to check as soon as Carla called to check to see if everything was alright. Andi was gone.

"At 8:20 that night, the sheriff's office received a phone call that Andi was missing, and the sheriff will tell you when and how the search began. He responded to the call. After interviewing everybody, the sheriff will tell you, at the time, he didn't know if Andria had run away or not. According to the family, that was uncharacteristic, no problems. Was it a stranger abduction? It happens. The sheriff will tell you the thought processes that he and some other officers went through. Was it somebody she knew? They didn't know. She just disappeared.

"The FBI was called in. They had a new program called FAST START, where they start on these things as quickly as possible. The state police sent every available investigator they had, many community volunteers. They all began looking. People were interviewed, people with red trucks. Karl Roberts was interviewed. 'Don't know, haven't seen her since last weekend.' He was right there helping to look for her the whole time."

A loud sob echoed through the courtroom. I looked up and noticed that even the reporters were wiping tears. I could not bear to look at my family. I could hear them sniffling. Again, I couldn't look in my mother's eyes. I reached over and took her hand.

"On Monday, May 17, no one knew what had happened to Andi; she was still missing, everyone was still looking. About 3 o'clock in the afternoon, Karl Roberts was subjected to another interview, and he volunteered to come talk with FBI Special Agent Mark Jessie and State Police Investigator Ocie Rateliff, and only then is when he told them what really happened to Andi."

Williamson cleared his throat.

"About 6:30 PM, May 17, Mr. Roberts gave them directions to where they could find the body. Agents and officers will testify how they then went to that deserted clear-cut. They found everything just as Uncle Karl had said it was. The crime scene was worked, photographs were taken, standard procedures at that time, investigative procedures occurred. The State is not going to show you a lot of technical work that was done on this case, but you will hear from Terry Rolf, DNA analyst at the crime lab, to show you that the shirt Karl Roberts was wearing that day, a relatively new shirt purchased Thursday, prior to the day Andi was missing. And there were some samples taken off that shirt, and her blood was on his shirt, is what the DNA analyst will testify to. Dr. Erickson from the crime lab will come, talk to you about the autopsy he performed on Andi and render his opinion to you. The State must prove its case beyond a reasonable doubt, and we have to prove to you the facts that constitute what's in this criminal information that the Defendant's been charged. We have to prove to you beyond a reasonable doubt that the Defendant committed rape with Andria Nichole Brewer and in the course of and furtherance of that rape or immediate flight therefrom, Karl Douglas Roberts caused the death of Andria Nichole Brewer under circumstances manifesting in extreme indifference to the value of human life. Thank you for your job as jurors, ladies and gentlemen."

He finished.

"Thank you, Mr. Williamson," Judge Ford said. "Mr. Hendry, Mr. Blount, you may make opening statements on behalf of the defendant."

Blount stood and casually walked to the front of the jury box. Running his fingers through his hair, he began.

"Thank you, Your Honor. May it please the Court, counsel, ladies and gentlemen of the jury. Again, my name is Darrel Blount. I'm from Mount Ida. Along with my co-counsel, I'll be representing Karl Roberts. The first thing I want to do is thank you all for being here. This is not a pleasant thing to do, it's not something we want to do, but without you being willing to sit as jurors, we wouldn't have a system. *You* are the ultimate people who will decide the guilt or innocence of Karl Douglas Roberts."

He paused and scratched his chin. "Now, Mr. Williamson has told you that the State will have to prove certain things beyond a reasonable doubt. Ladies and gentlemen, I'm not going to stand here before you and tell you that I don't think the State can meet its burden of proof because I do. I think the State will meet its burden of proof in at least a couple of those areas. But, the State must meet its burden of proof *and* show or assume that Karl Roberts, at the time that this act was committed, was competent to make the decision to do this act, to realize that what he was doing was wrong and in realizing this to be able to conform his actions to the requirements of the law. The burden is upon us to show you that Karl was not, in fact, competent at the time that this happened."

I couldn't believe my ears. Uncle Karl is a man who had held the same job for years, a husband and father to two children. This was a cold-hearted, premeditated crime. Her blood is on his shirt. Her blood is on his hands.

"There's one person I'd like you to consider that I think pretty much everyone has forgotten in this case. That person is a twelve-year-old boy that the evidence will show was riding his bicycle one day, some twenty years ago, and was hit by a dump truck." Blount stopped and pointed his finger towards Karl, who was keeping his head down, working hard to appear mentally challenged.

"When he was hit, the left side of his head, the evidence will show, was crushed. He was in a coma for a few days, and when he came out of that coma, this quiet, unassuming, good kid became a belligerent, combative boy of twelve. His personality had changed 180 degrees. From that day forth, he was not the Karl Roberts that his parents had known. He was totally changed. We'll have evidence that this is not uncommon. It's been known since way back in the middle of the nineteenth century. I think one of the names that you will probably hear from at least two experts today will be that of Phineas Gage. I want you to remember that name."

Phineas Gage was a 25-year-old foreman on a railroad construction job in September of 1848. His job involved the use of explosives to clear the way for a new track. Part of the task involved packing the explosive charge into drilled holes with a tamping iron. An accidental spark ignited the charge prematurely and sent the iron rod through Mr. Gage's skull. The meter-long shaft entered under his left cheekbone and exited through the top of his skull, landing thirty yards away. He keeled over, had a seizure, and then regained consciousness. With the help of colleagues, he was taken to a local doctor who cleansed the wound. Phineas Gage survived, but he was a changed man. Before the accident, Gage was well-liked and considered to be an honest, dependable, church-going man. After the accident, he was quick-tempered, arrogant, and used profuse profanity. He was dismissed from his job by the company that had previously regarded him as "the most efficient and capable" of their employees.

Gage lost the sight in his left eye. According to his doctor, "the balance between his intelligence and animal propensities" had injured his right frontal lobe. This case proved how a man's personality depends on the activity of the frontal lobe of the brain.

I never realized that a man named Phineas Gage, injured in a blast nearly 200 years ago, would be repeatedly compared to a confessed child killer when Phineas himself had never murdered anyone. But we heard all about Phineas Gage over and over. The defense team informed the jury that his injury was parallel to Karl's. It was ludicrous because Phineas Gage's personality changed immediately; Karl Roberts supposedly took twenty years.

Blount continued. "We will bring two experts to testify that they have examined Karl and that he has been given an MRI, and at the time this act was committed, ladies and gentlemen, a large chunk of his brain was missing. It's gone. It is not there. You cannot use something you do not have, and Karl does not have part of his frontal lobe. Karl took the life of a twelve-year-old girl. The seeds of this act were sown twenty years ago. You might say her fate was preordained; the evidence will show before she was even born."

The entire courtroom gasped in disbelief. Anger stabbed through my trembling body. Loud sobs came from the back of the courtroom.

"Order," the judge pounded the gavel. "The crowd will remain silent throughout these proceedings."

Blount continued, "Karl's IQ is in the borderline retarded range; depending on which end of the scale you look at, he could either be high retarded or low borderline. He also exhibits symptoms consistent with schizophrenia. He also saw and heard things that were not there. He's seen his wife at various times in different places that she could not have been, but he saw her, and to Karl, it was as real as me looking at all of you here now. We have experts that will tell you that due to his injuries, Karl has a very decreased ability to conform his actions as required by law. What that means very simply, ladies and gentlemen, is that he sees something, and he knows it's wrong, but unlike you and me, once he knows it's wrong, he cannot conform his actions; even knowing it's wrong, he can't stop."

The jury stared at Blount, not giving a hint as to what they were thinking. They sat solemn-faced, hands folded neatly in their laps.

"He knew what he was doing was wrong that day, and the evidence will show that. It will show that from his own statement, but his *injured* brain would not send the signal for him to stop. The evidence will show that an injury to the brain can manifest itself in different ways, and it mostly depends on what part of the brain sustained the injury. Sort of like if you put your hand on the stove and it's hot. You think my hand is burning and remove it. Someone like Karl would leave his hand there and let it burn. Another expert will testify that Karl suffers from dementia due to a head injury. I think we have all heard of dementia as senility or that a person can't get enough oxygen to the brain, and they do bizarre things that are out of character for them. We've heard of people with Alzheimer's disease. Alzheimer's is a form of dementia. We all know of people who have been good, law-abiding citizens all their life. Then, they are struck with Alzheimer's, and they do things that are inappropriate. They may take their clothes off and go walking down the street. Again, it's a form of dementia because a part of the brain isn't working. Karl's ability to control his behavior was significantly impaired by his injury. If Karl's brain had not been injured, he would not have committed this act. That is possibly the most important statement that you will hear on the witness stand. Absent the injury, he would not have done this act. Due to his injury, he was unable to conform his actions to the law."

Blount continued about the brain injury and the experts that would be brought in to confirm the defense's position that Karl was "retarded." That he didn't know what he was doing when he killed Andi.

Heartache settled around me as I heard things about my young daughter that no parent should ever have to hear.

"Ladies and gentlemen, it's very, very tragic that *this* young girl, this twelve-year-old girl died," he said without emotion.

This girl...

"Nobody is going to argue that. But, to convict Karl, you need to be convinced beyond a reasonable doubt that he had the ability to conform his actions to the law. I believe you will agree with me that you can't hold a person criminally responsible for something that he does not have the ability due to a brain injury to do any more than you can hold an Alzheimer's patient responsible or a stroke victim responsible for the fact that he can't move his arm. You'll agree, I believe, it is the same type of injury, the same type of problems. Thank you. The defense rests."

Next, the prosecutor called Sheriff Mike Oglesby to the stand and asked him to explain the events that happened the night of May 15, 1999. Oglesby detailed the 911 call that came into the Sheriff's Department in which Trina Roberts called, stating that her 12-year-old niece, Andi, was missing. Sheriff Oglesby arrived at the Brewer's house at about 8:40 PM. He began an initial investigation and thought that he was dealing with a runaway. But as the night progressed, he had a gut feeling that this case was more because Andi did not have a history of running away.

He described that on Sunday, May 16, he called the FBI and Arkansas State Police in on the case because Andi had not been seen or heard from since her disappearance. The only clue they had was the description of a red pickup truck. There were only two red pick-ups in the area; one belonged to Karl Roberts, the other to Bobby Stone.

The prosecution rested, and the defense passed on the witness.

The next witness called by the state was Lynn Benedict with the Arkansas State Police, who recounted the interrogation of Karl Roberts. This was a very difficult part of the trial for me because of Benedict's explanation. Prosecutor Williamson introduced the crime scene photos and asked if these were the photographs taken by him.

"Yes," he answered.

Next, Williamson asked him about picture number one. Mr. Benedict held the photograph up for the entire courtroom to see. It was a photograph of the lower half of Andi's body in the weeds. I felt vomit in the back of my throat, and in the peripheral part of my vision, dark clouds gathered and moved in towards me. I began to feel weak and woozy.

Am I going to pass out?

Those were the same little feet that I had kissed and nuzzled.

The legs that had kicked me in the womb. And there they were lying in the weeds, thrown away like trash. It was not just the photograph of a body. It was my baby. My flesh and blood.

I have to get out of here. I am on the verge of a panic attack.

I rushed out of the courtroom and down the stairs to the bathroom. Mom followed me out of the courtroom, and I let my eyes lock with hers for the first time in a long time. We sat there together and cried. I decided that I was not going back into the courtroom that day, which was probably best because next, they called the doctor who performed the autopsy on Andi. Jurors cried as they looked at the photographs of the crime scene.

While I was gone, the defense team tried to prove that Andi had consensual sex with Karl. That she had enticed him, a notion that Williamson quickly objected to.

With day one behind us, we went back to the hotel room, and I went to bed without dinner.

No way can I eat.

CHAPTER 17
THE TRIAL
DAY TWO

Being back in the courtroom for the second day of trial was strenuous. The courtroom bench was hard and cold. I brought a seat cushion to sit on during the remainder of the proceedings. The stress and discomfort were taking their toll. I was tired; I wanted this to be over with, I wanted to go back to Oklahoma. One thing that was particularly hard was being away from home. At a time when I needed familiar surroundings, I had to stay in a motel. I longed for my own bed; sleep was absent.

Colleen and her mom arrived back in court with us again. Every day, they drove an hour and a half one way to attend the trial. I knew it was hard on them. I was so glad they were there for me and my family. When something was said in court that upset me and I cried, Colleen sent an encouraging note to me from the back of the courtroom. During one difficult part of the trial, one of her notes read, "Satan's Spawn," in reference to a caption I had placed on Karl's photo on a blog I had started about Andi. I couldn't help but smile at her insight into my feelings about Karl.

That day proved to be interesting. The defense had hired an expert witness, Dr. Lee Archer, a well-respected neurologist who informed the jury that because of Karl's brain injury, it would be impossible for him to conform his actions to the law.

"He was missing 15 percent of his brain, part of his left frontal lobe. Without this portion, Karl was not capable of controlling his behavior. The same was true for his temper, which flared frequently," he said.

He also spoke of Karl's fits of anger toward his wife, during which he had choked her five times, once to the point of unconsciousness. Dr. Archer testified that Karl had told him he had killed Andi because he was angry with Greg's mother, Ann, for suggesting that the two families vacation together. Karl apparently had wanted to take a vacation with his own family, not with his mother-in-law. We found out later that he never mentioned this to the state doctor who examined him in October of 1999, but he had found it relevant to tell the defense's doctor in February of 2000.

After rigorous cross-examination wherein he asked Archer about the stability of Karl's life—his job, his wife, his children—Williamson asked a few questions that debunked everything the defense had tried to prove about Karl being mentally handicapped.

"In your opinion, the trigger for Karl's behavior on May 15, 1999, was the vacation incident? That was what set him off?"

"That's the way I understood it," Archer replied.

"Andi, at the point when he became enraged over the vacation plans, was a good quarter-mile distance away."

"Yes."

"Based upon the behavior that you've looked at with this particular defendant, when he lost control in the past, was that immediate loss of control in response to the stimuli he was faced with then?"

"Well, at least it starts, yes, immediately starts."

"You would say then, based upon your study and review of this defendant, he got angry at his mother-in-law Ann, and that was the trigger?"

"Yes," Archer replied.

"That trigger event, how consistent was it then that this defendant would drive to a location for his niece—who was not involved in this argument—put her in his truck and drive an additional 9.3 miles over a 12-to-13-minute period, rape her, then kill her, hide the body, then dispose of the evidence? But let's take that episode. How consistent was that with any other episode he had ever had in the past that had that length of duration?"

"I know nothing like that he ever did in the past," Archer

said.

He went on answering questions of that nature. There were no solid answers about behavior that caused a person to commit a heinous act some twenty years after an injury. Archer went forward, saying that the type of brain injury Karl had was the reason he choked his wife and struggled with a jealousy problem. He spoke of how that person would create disturbances in public places—church, shopping, public meetings—unable to control their behavior in everyday life. Karl had presented with none of these problems. He had been able to control himself.

Williamson finished.

"Would major behavioral difficulty, in your opinion, be that you couldn't attend family functions because you became overly excited or agitated about the ongoing family event?"

"I think that would be a major disability for that person."

"In the instance of Karl Roberts, the only evidence of a major behavioral difficulty would be the previous incidents regarding when he choked his wife?"

"Well, let's see, he was arrested once. He had all the behavior in the state hospital. His parents cited all the examples of when he became agitated and had difficulty calming down, so I guess there were a number of spells where he has documented behavior profiles."

"Would those things be examples of someone who could be

considered as having a *hot temper?"* the prosecutor asked, looking straight into his eyes.

"Yes, you could say that."

"If you had the type of injury that Mr. Roberts had, would you be a doctor today?"

"No," Dr. Archer answered.

"If you had the type of injury Mr. Roberts had, would you rape and murder your 12-year-old niece?" he asked.

"I would certainly hope not," Archer replied with a look of perplexity. His face flushed pink when Williamson said he had no further questions.

The next witness for the defense, Dr. Mary Weatherby, a neuropsychologist, fumbled her way to the witness stand. She rambled for over an hour about frontal lobe injuries. The jury was noticeably bored by her lecture, fidgeting in their chairs and glancing at their watches. One woman was even filing her nails. It wasn't until Weatherby attempted to dehumanize Andi that the jury sat up and took notice.

"Dr. Weatherby, in your report, you state that you talked to Karl Roberts about this incident and what happened immediately after it happened?"

"Yes."

"What did he tell you he did?"

"He said that he was raping her. He raped her. Then after he raped her, he thought, oh no, I'm in trouble. Okay, what am I going to do? I guess I will choke her. After he choked her, he ran to his truck; he decided that he better go back. He ran back and tried to give her CPR, which he had learned to do with a volunteer fire academy."

The courtroom gasps loudly. It was the first time we had heard anything of the sort. Karl had not told anyone except his defense team he had tried to resuscitate Andi.

Liar.

Weatherby continued as though she didn't hear the loud exasperation from the audience. "He didn't remember how to do it. So, he decided to proceed from there. 'Well, I guess I will cover her up with leaves.'"

"So, you are saying his organized thinking was not good?"

"Right, that is what I am saying."

She then went on to talk about the many times Karl choked his wife. Creating a defense for him that was unrealistic, trying to prove he was psychotic, saying he saw things in the jail that weren't there. It was obvious what the defense was trying to do—they were trying to convince the jury to let Karl go out on an insanity plea.

After Dr. Weatherby's testimony, we took a break for lunch. Williamson approached us before we left.

"If it's okay with all of you," he said, pointing to us. "I am not even going to cross-examine Dr. Weatherby—she's a nut job. The jury lost interest in her half an hour ago while she rambled on and on about nothing. The only thing she did was insult Andi. I have nothing to say to her, and that will say a lot."

We agreed with his reasoning and when Williamson passed on cross-examining her, the defense team looked noticeably shocked. Her testimony was so irrelevant the newspaper reporters didn't even mention her in the paper. In my opinion, she was the defense's biggest mistake. They began rustling through notes, wondering what they had done wrong. They pushed their heads toward Karl and talked with him in hushed tones.

The State placed Dr. Reginald Rutherford, a clinical neurologist, on the stand.

Williamson asked about his credentials before moving on to the bulk of the testimony.

"Doctor, would you explain to the jury whether or not you're familiar with injuries to the brain involving the frontal lobe."

"I am."

For several minutes, he explained the anatomy and functions of the brain and injuries to the brain. He agreed with the defense on several points regarding the frontal lobe but rejected several others.

"I really don't know why this happened. I can't make any sense of it. I've heard nothing today that clarifies in my mind why this has happened.

"The triggering event as testified to by Dr. Archer and also Dr. Weatherby about the discussion of a vacation, do you assess any validity to that?" Williamson said.

"It doesn't make sense to me. If this fellow has such a hair trigger, why did it take twenty years for that trigger to be pulled? If Karl was so close to the edge, then why did it take so long for something to happen? If he was so angry at his mother-in-law, why didn't he strangle her?" he asked matter-of-factly.

"In the course of your practice, how common is it to see persons have a great lapse in time between these behavioral events in their lives that suffer from a frontal lobe disorder?"

"Well, this is the exact opposite of what you would expect. You would expect things to be worse in the immediate period after the accident, to improve over time. You wouldn't expect delayed gross behavior or deterioration. That doesn't fit with clinical neurology in terms of medical history."

"Do you agree with Dr. Archer in his opinion that the younger the brain injury occurs, the better the likelihood of more recovery down the road?"

"That's a well-established principle in neurology."

"Did you find it significant that Karl Roberts played the drums?"

"There was a statement made that he had severe motor deficits that came up on one of his tests. I don't think it is reasonable to make such an assessment for somebody that plays the drums. That requires a high degree of coordination dexterity, so if you can play a drum kit, you have significant motor skill function. That doesn't make any sense; it doesn't fit."

"Dr. Rutherford, Dr. Archer believed that the major behavioral difficulty was exhibited by the defendant on the five occasions he choked his wife over the last ten years. Could you give us your opinion on that?" Williamson asks.

"Well, I don't think that's normal behavior. But there's one other piece of information I did find interesting. It was the notion on one occasion that Mr. Roberts was choked by his father during an argument, so there could be some element of learned behavior."

"What is learned behavior?"

"That often you follow in the same footsteps of your relatives."

It went on from there, with both sides feuding over whether Karl knew what he was doing or not. They made jabs at each other over Karl's missing brain portion. One side arguing that he was another Phineas Gage, the other saying there was no comparison because Phineas Gage never killed anyone. And through this entire charade, one person was missing...Andi.

The one who had been brutally raped and murdered.

Karl's only hope was the possibility of convincing the jurors that he didn't know what he was doing and couldn't help himself. I didn't think the jury was buying it, but I couldn't tell for sure. They were a bit stoic and hard to read. They kept solemn faces, but they were watching Karl, watching every move he made. For the most part, he sat with his head down, but a few times conferred with his attorneys when something was said that he didn't like. He was no dummy. He knew exactly what was happening and it didn't look good for him.

CHAPTER 18
THE TRIAL
DAY THREE

The day began with the state calling Danny Davis, Karl's former boss, to the witness stand. He was the owner of Mine Creek Construction. Davis stated that Karl had been his steadiest hand he'd had in thirty-three years of business—always punctual, never fighting with other employees or causing any kind of trouble. The defense wanted to prove that Karl was unable to perform his job because of his brain injury. When it was time for the defense to cross-examine, Daryl Blount took center stage.

"Mr. Davis, is it true that Karl Roberts was never left unattended on the job and always had a supervisor around when he was working?" Blount asked.

"Yes, that's true, as did everyone working on my crew," Davis answered.

"Could Karl be trusted to do the layout plans for the

bridgework?" he asked.

"No."

"Would you agree with me that Karl was unable to perform at his highest ability because he couldn't do the layout plans?" Blount spouted.

"I am usually the one who does these plans because they are very difficult; not very many people are able to do them at all," Davis said.

The defense rested.

Next, the state called William Padgett. He lived next door to the elder Brewers. Padgett was the last person to see Andi alive. He had been driving home from a fishing trip on May 15, 1999, when he met Karl driving down the road leading away from the Brewer residence. Karl had almost run Padgett into the ditch. Karl waved and then drove on. Nothing seemed particularly abnormal except that Karl had almost run him off the road. He noticed the top of a small head peering above the dash, which he now knew had been Andi. Initially, he had thought it was Karl's 4-year-old daughter. Karl must have been holding her down in the seat or shoving her into the floorboard. This particularly disturbed him.

He approached me during a break from court proceedings.

"I feel terrible; if I had only known it was Andi, I could have saved her. I would not have let him take her away," he stated, shaking his head. "I would have saved her," God knows I would have," he said, wiping tears from his eyes.

"I know you would have," I said.

"I was the last one to see her alive."

We embraced. He was especially upset. I didn't know how to make him feel better because I was struggling myself. Later, Padgett would recall the words that Karl had spoken to him during the search for Andi.

"So, you say you saw me the other day," Karl had asked almost threateningly.

"Yes, I did," Padgett answered.

"No, you didn't," Karl replied, turning and walking away.

Perry Barrett was next. He had worked for a propane company in and around the Cove area. He had known Karl since high school. He was doing his route on May 15, 1999, and noticed Karl at the car wash just after dusk, spraying the bottom of his truck.

"It seemed odd to me how he was leaned over spraying the bottom of his pick-up," he stated.

"What was odd about washing his vehicle in that manner? Haven't you ever washed your truck, Mr. Barrett?" Blount asked sarcastically.

"Yes, but I have never bent over to spray the underside of my truck. I noticed it because it looked odd," he replied.

The final witness for the state was Dr. Charles Mallory, a

state psychologist. Dr. Mallory had interviewed Karl in October of 1999 at the state hospital in Little Rock, Arkansas. Dr. Mallory testified that Karl had never mentioned to him that the reason he had killed Andi was because he was angry with his mother-in-law, Ann, about taking a family vacation.

"If he were out of control or acting like an animal because of a brain defect, what happened would have happened right there. Instead, he picked a time when he knew no one would be home with Andi. This did not appear to be an accident. He made note that Greg was not at home. He said something came over him, that he knew he had to go get Andi, but despite this possible compulsion, he was able to take steps – that is, he waited to rape her. This all indicated he could refrain, and he had the capacity to control his behavior," the doctor stated.

He also testified that Karl had admitted that he was not sexually attracted to Andi, but two months prior to her death, he had found that he wanted to look up her dress at a family gathering. He couldn't stop thinking about her.

The courtroom gasped again at this new information. It appalled everyone to know that Karl had had these fantasies about Andi.

Once again, the defense and prosecution argued back and forth as the jury looked on. I wanted to know what they were thinking. Were they buying all this stuff about a "special" little boy who had been run over by a dump truck? Did they believe that his brain had malfunctioned and caused him to snap some twenty years after his injury?

Or did they think he was a cold-blooded killer who had preyed on a child?

THE TRIAL
DAY FOUR

We arrived at the courthouse for the closing arguments. Once again, we were blinded by the bright lights from the television crews. Colleen stayed close by my side and was very proficient at protecting me from the media. This certainly would be the top story on the news again that night in the state of Arkansas. That day was the final day of the trial. Karl would either be convicted or exonerated. I was not worried about a not-guilty verdict. The facts were plain to see. He had committed the crime. He had admitted to doing it.

In the closing part of the trial, both attorneys explained what they were asking the jury to do. The prosecution was seeking a conviction of capital murder, for which they would later have to decide the punishment during the sentencing phase—life without parole or death. The defense was asking the jury to acquit Karl on grounds that he had not been able to conform his actions to the law because of his brain injury.

Prosecutor Williamson for the State of Arkansas began.

"May it please the counsel, ladies and gentlemen of the jury, this is the day we've been waiting to get to," he stated, going briefly over the jury information sheet. "I do not believe there is reasonable doubt in this case. There is absolutely no doubt as to what Karl Roberts did to his niece, Andria Brewer. He confessed to it," Williamson paced in front of the jury box with a photograph of Andi strategically placed on the backside of the papers he was holding. Her smiling face was staring at them.

"He confessed to raping her, and then he confessed to choking, strangling her to death. He confessed to it. He did not just do it in a flash, an impulse, or an instant, but he drove her 9.3 miles to a secluded area into a location where there were no other people around. There was *no one* to hear her scream or cry for help."

I put my head in my hands and leaned down. I cried so many tears they formed a small puddle at my feet. I wept silently. Williamson had asked us to try to hold our emotions so as not to influence the jurors, but I had never cried like that before.

He continued, "He's her uncle, and he has taken her into a clear-cut. There's no place where it says define to the jury what it means to be under circumstances manifesting extreme indifference to the value of human life. But, ladies and gentlemen, I don't know what a more compelling definition of extreme indifference to the value of human life would be than what you have seen and heard in this case. I would say that this Defendant was *extremely* indifferent to the value of Andi Brewer's life. She wanted to know where they were going—he told her to shut up. When they got there, she asked him what he was going to do to her. And he told her using words that a 12-year-old shouldn't have to hear. And then not only did he tell her, but he also forced her to have sexual intercourse with him. He forced her to the ground. He forced off her panties, and he raped her. And then, like so many other things in our society that are disposed of, when he was finished with her, he got rid of her. What other reason would he have choked her to death? It was because he didn't need her anymore; he was through with her. Just like a sack of trash, he drug her out in the woods and covered her up so no one could find her. But, before he did that, he wanted to make sure there weren't any other identifiers with her body, so he was sharp enough to remove the clothes that could identify her. He cleaned up his crime area and threw her clothes in the creek and then was off to Momma and Daddy's house to drink coffee. That is extreme indifference to the value of human life."

Williamson's face was blood red.

"Now, we have covered the rape part; we have covered the extreme indifference to the value of human life because I can't think of a better example of going completely indifferent to what her life was worth. He didn't have to kill her. He could have raped her, and he could have left her alive. He could have said it was all a lie. She doesn't know what she's saying; someone else came and got her. He's real good at making up stories as to what happened, and he's perfectly capable of having done that. He could have completely denied that. Because she might not have told, or if she told, they might not have believed her. There are a lot of things that could have happened. He didn't have to kill her. Why did he do it? Because her life to him was not worth anything. That, ladies and gentlemen, in Arkansas, is capital murder, and that's what you need to look at, and you all need to make a decision that is beyond a reasonable doubt. We have proved these elements."

Next, Williamson touched on the highlights of the trial: Karl's good work ethic, his family life, the frontal lobe injury, allegedly choking his wife, and the alcohol he had consumed that day. He ended with testimony from FBI special agent Mark Jessie.

"I remember one thing Mark Jessie said, how Karl acted when he spoke with him; Karl stated that he had ruined his life in ten minutes. Not thinking about the rest of Andi's life. And don't see Karl as a living, breathing creature who can't carry a stick of wood from one side of the pile to another. His employer said he's the best hand he'd ever had and made $50,000.00 the last year he worked for him. This ain't Phineas Gage, this is Karl Roberts. He killed his niece after he finished raping her."

"Thank you, Mr. Williamson," Judge Ford said. "Mr. Blount, on behalf of your client."

"Thank you, Your Honor," he stood and faced the jury. "May it please the Court, counsel, ladies and gentlemen of the jury. The first thing I want to do is thank you all for being here, thank you for your attention. I told you in opening statements that we don't deny that Karl took the life of Andria Brewer. There has been ample testimony that you can find that Karl committed this act. Andria Brewer was strangled; she was strangled so that the supply of blood to her brain was cut off long enough to cause unconsciousness and death. It was testified that unconsciousness could occur in about 15 to 20 seconds, maybe a little less if both sides were cut off. Andria was sexually assaulted, and this left bruising consistent with a first sexual experience or forcible rape. This was the only bruising on her body; she wasn't beaten, she wasn't tortured, and the only cuts on her body were scratches from the drag marks that occurred after her death. Her injuries, absent from the strangulation, wouldn't have even caused a need for medical attention. Ladies and gentlemen, she was strangled to death, and Karl confessed. He led officers to her body, but as you were also told, you must find that Karl had the ability to conform his conduct to the requirements of the law. The prosecutor said he did. My friend, Mr. Williamson, is asking you to look at Karl as a rational, normal person, and that's not the case. You must not only be convinced beyond a reasonable doubt that Karl had the ability to know right from wrong and have the ability to conform his actions to the law. Mr. Williamson says he is not Phineas Gage; well, no, he's not. Phineas Gage died a long time ago. But Karl suffered a serious injury to his brain when he was twelve years old. In many ways, Karl is an adolescent. The question is, did the injury to Karl's brain twenty years ago cause him to be unable to control himself on May 15, 1999?"

He continued about the doctors and the frontal lobe injury

before ending.

"Due to Karl's mental disease or defect, he misperceives things. He doesn't see them like we do. Remember how I told you in opening statements that if I put my hand on a stove, I perceive it as hot, and I would remove it immediately? However, a person who misperceives things may put his hand on a stove and let it completely burn because he perceives it as being cold. If Karl is in a certain frame of mind, it could mean I want to fight, and he'll jump up and pop me in the nose, and he can't stop himself from doing that because he can't control his behavior. He misperceives things. Mr. Williamson is going to have the chance to get back up one last time and tell you that everything I have said is not true, that it is all smoke and mirrors, but the facts remain. A perfectly trivial comment by his mother-in-law, 'Wait and take your vacation because I will take mine and we'll all go together,' would have meant absolutely nothing to any of us, but Karl was infuriated, and we don't know why it infuriated a non-rational person who's missing a very large portion of their brain. We don't hold other victims of brain loss responsible, ladies and gentlemen. Therefore, I ask you now, I beg you now: don't hold Karl Roberts responsible because he lost part of his brain in 1980. If it hadn't been for the damage suffered in this accident, this incident would have never happened. Vote your conscience. Find Karl Roberts not guilty by reason of mental disease or defect. Thank you."

He sat down and began to rustle through the papers on the

table. Karl leaned over and whispered something to him. The jury noticed and stared at him; he didn't look their way.

"Thank you, Mr. Blount. Mr. Williamson, you may conclude on behalf of the State of Arkansas."

"Thank you, Your Honor," he shook his head and walked slowly to face the jury.

"A man has got part of his right frontal lobe gone. Mr. Blount wants to believe that if you've got fifteen percent of your car missing, it won't run. I submit that if all four fenders fall off that car, it'll still run. The doors can fall off, it'll still run. The trunk can fall off, it'll still run. The hood can fly off, it'll still run. The question is, is the engine working and the wiring okay? Does the car start in the morning? Let's look at this defendant. He's got brain damage. Does everyone who's got brain damage go out and rape and kill their niece? No. Does everyone with brain damage go out and commit crimes at all? No. Do people without brain damage go out and commit crime? Yes. So that fact right there doesn't mean squat.

"Karl's first opportunity to tell the whole truth was whenever he confessed to the police after two days of lies. 'I raped her, and I killed her, and I left her body in the woods these last two days while we've been looking for her.' That was his first time to tell the truth, but what did he do? He didn't mention anything about trying to go back and revive her; he didn't mention anything about being mad at his mother-in-law. He didn't mention any of that crap. Do you know why? Because it's not true. If he can't control himself, why didn't he choke the living daylights out of Ann Brewer? Because it didn't happen."

Williamson was angry again. "This man thought about what he was going to do, and he thought about it prior to that day. Remember what he told the FBI? Well, when I was going to the Brewer's house to play my drum set that afternoon, what did I notice? I noticed that Carla Brewer's car was at work like it usually is at the Hatfield Super Stop. What else did he note? That Greg Brewer usually fishes or hunts on Saturdays when he's not at work at U.S. Motors. He knew Greg was fishing. What did he say about Andi? He said Andi is usually at her grandparents' house or at home babysitting her brother and sister. He knew, ladies and gentlemen, where she was and what she would be doing, and there was nobody else there. And two months prior to this incident, he had seen her wearing a dress, and he had looked up her skirt. She was eleven at the time.

"Folks, I submit to you that he was thinking about this for a couple of months and just because he has brain damage doesn't mean he can't conform his conduct to the requirements of the law. A Phineas Gage, he's not. A man out of control of his emotions and his ability to conform to the law, he's not. But what is he? He's just like so many other people in our society today. 'It ain't my fault.' This is what it boils down to. The State has proven its case beyond a reasonable doubt. He raped her, and he killed her, and he's indifferent to the value of her little life. We've proven that. Have they proven by the preponderance of the evidence that he's got something wrong with him other than a brain injury? No. What has he proven? He's proven that in 10 minutes, he ruined his own life. That's what he's proven. He's proven that 'gee, it's not my fault, they should have done a better job at the hospital when I was hit by a dump truck twenty years ago.' Folks, it's his fault. He's personally accountable for this death, for this rape—this murder. Ladies and gentlemen, he's been found guilty; you need to find him guilty beyond a reasonable doubt of capital murder because that's what he has done. Thank you."

The sigh was audible. The audience had been holding their breath. A slight rustling began around the room, and voices could be heard talking in hushed tones.

"Thank you, Mr. Williamson."

The jurors were instructed on what to do, elect a foreman, and deliberate. They are excused at 10:45 AM to decide Karl's fate—they were back at 11:19. We barely had time to use the facilities and have a drink of soda.

"Ladies and gentlemen, I am advised that the jury has reached a verdict. I want to compliment and commend the audience for their behavior throughout this trial and I do appreciate it and ask you to continue in the same good manner. They are bringing the jury in shortly, and we will have a verdict."

The jury was ushered in. Police officers position themselves across the front of the courtroom for the verdict to be read.

"Let the record reflect that the defendant and his attorneys are present, the jury is seated. Has the jury reached a verdict with respect to the guilt or innocence of the defendant?" Judge Ford asked.

"We have, Your Honor," the jury foreman said.

"Would you hand the verdict form to the bailiff, please?"

The sheet of paper was taken from the foreman and handed to the judge.

"Ladies and gentlemen, I will now read and place into the record the verdict of the jury." He paused and adjusted his glasses.

"We, the jury, find Karl Douglas Roberts guilty of capital murder."

The courtroom erupted in cheers. It was like something that would have happened in the movies. The applause, whoops, and yells echoed the court. I thought the judge would rap his gavel and shout, 'Order in the court,' but he didn't.

Relief flooded my body. I knew Uncle Karl would never be free to hurt another child. The judge released everyone for lunch, instructing us to be back at 1:00 PM for the sentencing phase.

The prosecutor approached us with a smile of victory on his face.

"We are only halfway through," he stated. "Next is when you

all give your victim impact statement. Who's going to go first?" he asked.

"I will," I said.

"Okay, I just want to tell you that it will be very difficult. You will become emotional; it's a lot different than sitting out here. Can you do it?"

"Yes, I can." I nodded.

When Williamson called me to the stand, I was sworn in. Williamson introduced me and said, "Please read your statement to the jury."

I turned and faced the jury. I searched each face. I wondered if they could feel my pain and loss. I wondered if they knew the many nights I had cried myself to sleep, wondered if they knew I was dying inside. The faces stared back at me. I still could not read them.

My voice quivered as I read:

"The effects this brutal crime has had on me and my family are devastating. We have not only lost trust, understanding, and the ability to forgive, but we have lost a precious gift from God, a 12-year-old little girl who captured the heart of every person she met. Andi was a beautiful person who did not deserve the evil that befell her. She was a kind, loving, gentle soul who loved children and wanted to be a schoolteacher when she grew up, but she has been denied that privilege. Because of this horrendous crime, my

daughter not only lost her life, but she will never go to Jr. High or High School. She will never have a first date or a first kiss. She was denied her Senior Prom. Andi will never fall in love and get married. I will never hold my grandchildren from my first-born daughter because she has been murdered. I can only visit her at Six Mile Cemetery, where what remains of her is a 5-foot headstone marked with her name.

Twelve years is not living life to its fullest; twelve years was only the beginning for Andi, and she was robbed of a wonderful life. Andi was a modest child who would not have harmed a soul, once even compelling her stepfather, Kris, to go out in a thunderstorm to cover the neighbor's kennel with a plastic tarp because the dogs inside were getting drenched.

Andi loved her life and was a happy, well-adjusted child. She was a little girl whose smile and laughter demonstrated the innocence of who she was. I love and miss her desperately every day. My thoughts are never far from her, and weeping has become a daily occurrence. If only I could have done something to save her from the predator lurking in the family, but I didn't know. Now, I must live with thoughts and mental images of a crime so horrendous that even the toughest of law enforcement officers were brought to tears. I am tormented daily with thoughts of my little girl screaming for help with no one to hear her cries. I live nightly with the demons that torment my soul, screaming to me that I was not there to stop this, that I couldn't help my daughter the one time in her life that she needed me most. This crime has crushed my family into the dirt of society. People are uncomfortable around us and refuse to mention the crime to us for fear that we might fall into a heap. Andi was part of me; my blood pumped through her veins, and now, whenever I mention her, people shy away from the subject.

This crime has made us freaks, and we did nothing wrong. We tried our best to raise a little girl to adulthood and give her a normal life. Her normal life ended on May 15, 1999, when she was abducted out of the privacy of her home, raped, and strangled. She didn't deserve that; she was a beautiful person who deserved to grow up.

My sentencing recommendation for the defendant is the death penalty. He gave up his right to live a full life when he made the choice to abduct, rape, and murder a twelve-year-old girl. My lovely daughter wasn't given the chance to plead before a court of law for her life; instead, she was brutally murdered. The defendant does not deserve the sympathy of the court. He is the one who destroyed the lives of many people, including his own wife and children. The only one who deserves sympathy is Andi; she has suffered the most. Justice will not be served if the defendant is simply given life in prison. That says to others that it is okay to commit brutal sex crimes against children.

I wish each one of you here today could have had the privilege of knowing Andi; she was a wonderful human being who deserved to live. The defendant does not deserve life; we would all be better off if he were dead, the world would be rid of one more evil creature, and the citizens of Arkansas would be spared the expense of housing and feeding a confessed child killer. The death penalty is the only sensible solution in this case for the sake of all children, for the sake of the citizens of Arkansas and most of all for the sake of Andi. My daughter deserves to rest in peace, and the death of her killer would warrant that."

Finally, when all the statements had been read, the defense placed Karl's family on the stand to beg for his life. His sister spoke of how he had been different after his head injury. His mother begged for his life to be spared. She broke down and cried for him. It was all so sad. This crime had brutalized two families.

Karl's father, Bob, took the stand. He, too, begged for Karl's life, stating that he didn't know if he could take another death in their family. Karl's sister and nephew had died previously. Then Bob read a letter that Karl had written to everyone apologizing for his crime.

"I wish I could fix everything. I know you hate me. You have every right," Karl had written.

It was the first time there had ever been anything close to an apology, and I didn't know if Karl had written it or if his parents had done so to save his life.

Next, the defense team gave their closing arguments. Attorney Buddy Hendry withstood this task. Blount didn't stand before the jury again during the rest of the trial. It looked as though the defeat of capital murder had done him in. I felt as though he was pouting because he didn't win, but I couldn't say for certain. Hendry pleaded with the jury to spare Karl's life for the sake of his children and wife, for the sake of his elderly parents.

"Let the killing stop here," he pleaded. "You are the only ones who can have mercy on Karl."

Tim Williamson was ordered by Judge Ford to give closing arguments for the state of Arkansas. This was the big moment; Williamson was ready. His eyes were fiery-blue; he looked like a dragon slayer entering battle. He was poised, confident, and a little arrogant, *but not in a bad way.* This was his last chance to see that justice was served.

He had to prove to the jury that Andi had died in a cruel and depraved manner. With the 8x10 photograph of Andi smiling in his hand, he faced the jury and spoke slowly and methodically.

"This is all the proof of cruel and depraved you need, how Roberts ordered Andi into the truck and drove her to an overgrown, trash-cluttered logging trail as she begged for him to turn around and take her home, how Roberts told Andi what he was going to do to her in explicit, profane language and demanded that she remove her clothes. How he pressed his thumbs against her neck to kill her."

He reminded the jury that once Roberts began strangling her, it would have taken 20 seconds for her to lapse into unconsciousness, and it would have been another two minutes before she was dead.

"Cruel and depraved perfectly describes this crime if you think about the prolonged agony and torture of the victim.

"She's on her back, he's on top of her, and she's laying on briars, roots, rocks. What's 'prolonged' to a 12-year-old who's being raped by her uncle?

"Let's look at the clock—the second hand is at the top—and let's wait 2 minutes and 20 seconds."

The courtroom was silent.

Two Twenty. She is fighting, fighting for breath. Wriggling, trying to get away. Prying at the hands on her neck, scratching at the face looming up above her, two twenty. Images flash, her birth, saying mama, first steps, first Christmas, her hands, beautiful little hands, sweet little giggle, I'm scared, Mommy.

Two minutes, twenty seconds—long enough for more tears to spill out onto the wood floor between my feet.

"I think two minutes, twenty seconds is an eternity," Williamson whispered, voice cracking.

The jurors wiped their tears, and then they were released to decide Karl's fate. The reporters asked if I would mind giving a couple of interviews. I did and then waited and paced around the courtroom.

Forty-five minutes later, the jury was brought back in.

"Has the jury reached a decision?" the judge asked.

"Yes, Your Honor," the foreman said.

The bailiff handed the sentence to the judge. He opened it and cleared his throat. My heart was beating so loudly I could hear it.

"Mr. Roberts, you have been sentenced to die by lethal injection. A jury of your peers has judged you, but one day, there will be a greater judgment. May God have mercy on your soul."

"He already has," Karl spoke for the first time, seemingly taking one last jab at us. His mother burst out crying.

Gasp! What God did he serve?

There was no applause this time—only the sound of Karl's family sniffling and crying in the background.

The deputies handcuffed him and led him back to jail. Williamson approached us with a huge look of relief on his face. I hugged and thanked him for his hard work.

As I turned to walk out of the courtroom, I came face to face with Bob Roberts, Karl's dad. His face was red, and he was weeping. He tried to take me by the hand, and I uncomfortably pulled away. I stared into his eyes—so much hurt, so much pain.

Barely above a whisper, he said, "I didn't raise him to be this way. He wasn't raised like this, please believe me."

I felt panicky and wanted to run, but one of the officers

intervened and led me out of the courtroom.

Once outside, reporters surrounded us.

"Do you think you will ever be able to forgive Roberts for killing your daughter?"

I was stunned. In all the months of grieving, it was the first time I had even considered forgiveness. I didn't know how to answer her question.

"I don't know, God will have to figure that one out," I said.

I thought about that question all the way back to Tulsa. I didn't know when or if I could ever forgive. The only thing I knew for sure was that I felt justice had been served. I thought it would be over soon. He was a dead man.

Boy, was I ever wrong.

CHAPTER 19
A VOICE FOR THE VOICELESS

"You must always stand up and fight for your child. You are her voice now." ~ Colleen Nick

JULY 2000

The sign on the Union Bank in Mena, Arkansas, flashed 102 degrees. It was so hot that the birds weren't even chirping; I assumed they were hiding deep in the pine trees atop Rich Mountain, nestled in the Ouachitas. The sweltering heat caused the air conditioner in my car to work overtime. I had once again driven from Oklahoma to Arkansas, a three-hour trip, to attend another court hearing. Karl Roberts, now Arkansas Department of Corrections SK956, would give up his rights to appeal his conviction of capital murder, a conviction that carried the penalty of death for him.

It had been eight weeks since a jury had convicted him of the violent crime he had committed against Andi. Roberts had decided he wanted to die. To complete this process, he had to go before the court and request this motion because, in Arkansas, upon the conviction of death, there was an automatic appeal given whether it was wanted or not. Prosecutor Williamson had called me and told me that Roberts was done and that, according to his attorneys, he just wanted to die. The newspaper, of course, blasted his words on the front page.

Roberts: 'I want to die'

Convicted murderer Karl Roberts told the court last week that he wants to waive his appeals so that his death sentence can be served as soon as possible.

In a brief, 20-minute hearing, Roberts told the court room he is prepared to accept his sentence.

"I want to die," Roberts said.

"Are you telling me that you're asking that the death sentence be carried out?" Polk County circuit Judge Gayle Ford said.

"Yes," Roberts said.

While it seems clear that Roberts doesn't want to undergo the appeals process, it may not be that easy.

First of all, the Arkansas Supreme Court must review all death penalty trials before an actual execution date can be released.

Additionally, Roberts will most likely be subject to a competency trial to see if he has the mental capacity to determine his own fate.

Doctors testified earlier that Roberts had lost 15 percent of the frontal lobe of his brain in an accident when he was a child. The missing portion helps control reasoning and decision-making, expert witnesses testified.

The result of the accident left Roberts an adolescent in an adult's body, and made it difficult for Roberts to control his emotions, doctors said. Further, doctors testified that Roberts suffers from dementia, often hearing and seeing things which are not there.

On May 19, a jury found Roberts guilty of murdering his niece, Andi Brewer, and returned with the death penalty after 45 minutes of deliberation.

I had mixed emotions about this entire ordeal; on the one hand, the world would be rid of a violent child killer; on the other hand, he would get his wish—this was what he had wanted. He had not wished to sit on death row for years while faceless defense attorneys fought for what should have been taken away the day he had confessed to the murder. He had wanted to die as soon as possible. My thoughts about his demise were mixed because, according to his family, he had found God. Why hadn't he turned to God before he had killed Andi and spared us the torment of his selfish violence? Karl had never been a victim; it had been living hell. He had been given the right to choose life or death when Andi wasn't. Death had not been what she had wanted. She had wanted to live and grow up. I had so many unanswered questions, there were still so many sleepless nights; the torture of my soul continued forward.

Arriving at the prosecuting attorney's office with my mother, Ann, we parked and entered the building. Jo Mitchell greeted us. She had gotten so close to our family over the course of the previous year that she had to take a few weeks off from work after the trial to recover. It had been as though she had lost a loved one, too.

She also told me that her mother had attended a funeral in the cemetery where Andi was buried. She had told Jo about the grave with the enormous headstone and mountain of flowers.

"It is so noticeable that after the funeral, I walked to the grave and realized that it was the grave of the little girl who had been murdered," her mother had told her. "That little girl must have been loved."

"You have no idea how loved that child was," Jo had said.

Colleen Nick and her mother, Joanna, arrived at the prosecutor's office shortly after us. We all piled into Colleen's van and went to lunch before the one o'clock hearing. Colleen once again was showing her support to my family and Andi by attending the waiver of appeal hearing. I was very grateful that people cared about my daughter.

After lunch, we arrived at the courthouse to attend the hearing. Once again, we entered through the customary metal detector. The same deputy who had searched us during the trial was posted at the station. She smiled at us warmly as we walked through the detour and said, "You can go on in."

We entered the courtroom, and the feelings of helplessness washed over me again. This was the place where Karl had been convicted for killing my Andi. A place where I had heard the most heartbreaking things a parent could ever hear. The details of Andi's brutal murder were still fresh. My feelings took me by surprise. I felt the pain, rage, and desperation again. My heart flipped in my chest as the waves of grief once again surfaced. I took a deep breath and sat down in the place I had occupied during the murder trial.

Karl's wife and parents entered the courtroom and were seated on the defense side of the room. They sat stoically, never glancing our way. They weren't concerned with us or Andi, just Karl and his impending death. I wanted to shout at them. I wanted to take my wallet out of my purse and show them all the pictures I had of Andi and scream, "Look what he took from me. She will never grow past twelve."

But I didn't.

The deputies brought Karl to the courtroom. He was dressed in prison whites, his face was drawn and sullen, his black hair was peppered with gray, and his eyes were empty and emotionless. The stress of prison life had taken a toll on him. He waved and smiled at his wife and parents and took his seat at the defense table.

The judge entered, and the court was declared to be in session. The defense asked Karl to take the stand. He stood, was sworn in, and took his seat on the witness stand.

His lawyer, Buddy Hendry, stood at the microphone behind the attorney table and began to ask Karl questions.

"Mr. Roberts, do you understand that by waiving your right to an appeal that your sentence of death will be carried out?"

"Yes," Karl answered.

"Are you taking any medications or under the influence of alcohol at this time?"

"No."

He finished with similar yes or no questions. Next, Judge Ford asked the prosecutor, Tim Williamson, if he had any questions. Tim said no.

"Are you telling me that you're asking that the death sentence be carried out?" Judge Ford asked.

"Yes, I want to die," Karl answered.

These words stuck with me all the way back to Oklahoma.

I thought about Karl Roberts and his family the entire trip. His parents, Bob and Peggy, had been upstanding citizens in the community before Andi's murder. Now, the whispers of small-town gossip kept them feeling isolated and alone. I had heard that they had quit going to church.

"He wasn't raised that way."

Did that matter now? I didn't know. I just wanted my daughter back. To hell with how Karl Roberts was raised; whatever they had done, it hadn't worked. He was a cold-blooded child killer, of that, I was sure.

CHAPTER 20
AUGUST 2000

The line of parents and children stretched all the way across the gymnasium floor and out the front. Kris waded through the crowd and told me the line stretched around the building. We had been working with several businesses and local law enforcement in area towns to fingerprint and photograph children in memory of Andi. The response was phenomenal. Doing several media appearances on local television stations and telling Andi's story brought people out in masses. It was a family effort coupled with a passionate businessman, Michael Watson. Michael had photographed and fingerprinted children for years and, prior to Andi's abduction and murder, had utilized the help of the Owasso Fire Department, Kris' place of employment. For years, Kris had assisted Michael with fingerprinting and photographing young ones; when Michael realized Kris' stepdaughter had been kidnapped, he was shocked and wanted to help create a legacy for her. We set out on a campaign to make children safer and equip their parents with the information and knowledge of what to do if their child was ever abducted.

I arranged the table, and we began working. Most days, two to three hundred children would come through. Making sure their parents received their fingerprints and the safety information, we informed them what to do if their child went missing. We were empowering our community in Andi's name. Standing on our feet for hours, hands covered in ink, we accomplished a great feat. The campaign, which lasted about a year, resulted in over 15,000 children being fingerprinted, and as many DNA kits were passed out. I spoke to nearly as many about the issues of being safe— sometimes in small daycares or churches, other times to parents or the media. I created a website and became a volunteer with the National Center for Missing Children. I felt better about myself, and the devastating grief eased while I stayed busy. Things came rushing back to me later that month when two small girls from a Tulsa suburb were kidnapped from the driveway they had been playing in.

That Saturday night, Kris and I had taken the girls to a relative's house. We grilled steaks and swam in their pool. Kristin and Melanie played with their 7-year-old cousin. Samantha, a petite girl with long dark hair, had just recently learned how to swim. Swimming like a fish, she dove under the water like a mermaid with her long black hair flowing behind her. All three girls were having a blast. I watched as they giggled and splashed around.

Miles away in a suburb west of Tulsa on this same Saturday night, another 7-year-old girl was playing outside with her 12-year-old neighbor. They were most likely enjoying the end of summer—happy it was the weekend, as school had started the previous Thursday. The girls, minding their own business, were not aware of the predator lurking nearby. Suddenly, he appeared, snatched both away, and disappeared into the dusk. When the mother of the 7-year-old stepped outside to check on the girls, they were gone, nowhere to be found. She panicked and rushed around madly, trying to locate them. Finally, she called 911.

The responding officers prayed for the best but feared the worst, hoping the girls had wandered off and lost track of time. But they feared the girls had been abducted. Searching near the disappearance site, the police department called the fire department to mount a massive town search for the missing girls. Three hours passed as search teams paraded the streets of the small Oklahoma town in search of the two. They knocked on doors, looked behind bushes, searched ditches and parked cars. There was no sign of them. Finally, they approached an abandoned house. The party knocked on the door and then burst through it when they heard a scream. To their sheer horror, they found the abductor with the girls. The 7-year-old had been strangled and was dead; the other had been repeatedly sexually assaulted but was still alive. The man who had taken them was a 19-year-old repeat juvenile sex offender who was not registered as a sex offender because all his offenses had occurred before he was 18. After the death of the 7-year-old, several Oklahoma lawmakers created the Oklahoma Juvenile Sex Offender Law, requiring violent juvenile sex offenders to register. It upset me that it took the death of that beautiful girl for such a law to be put into effect.

I didn't hear about the case until the next day when I read the newspaper. I wept for the two families of these innocent children. My heart was broken for the surviving girl. I cried for the child who had perished. I wanted to reach out to these families, but I didn't know how. I called Colleen at the Morgan Nick Foundation and poured my heart out to her. She told me that she would call the police department and try to offer support to the families through the efforts of the Morgan Nick Foundation and Team HOPE. Neither family received the message of our desire to help.

Feeling desperate to reach out to the mother of the 7-year-old, I wrote her a letter from my heart, a letter in the same fashion Marc Klaas had written me. When I began writing, things flowed out of my heart that I never believed could come from my soul. I told her that I knew the road she was walking, and I was available to listen if she wanted to contact me day or night. I realized the difference between being compassionate to someone and being moved with compassion. I was moved with compassion for this woman whom I had never met. I could feel her pain and agony. I could see the desperation in her eyes on the evening news. I wanted to take her in my arms and hug her. I knew her pain would become much greater in the future as the shock of the crime wore off.

Later that week, I took flowers and the letter to the funeral home in honor of Andi and in memory of the small child who had suffered a similar fate. Wanting to show her family that I cared and was deeply grieved for what they were going through. I knew the victimization wouldn't end when they placed the child in the grave. I knew that it was only the beginning of a nightmare for them. I picked out a huge pink bouquet of flowers—pink carnations and pink roses to represent innocence. I paid for the flowers, and when I smelled the roses, the scent took me back to the funeral of my own child. My stomach began to churn, and I fought to keep the tears back.

I drove to the suburban town about a half hour away. My heart pounded heavily in my chest when I parked at the funeral home. I turned off the car. I was scared to go in.

I took a deep breath and opened the car door. I spilled some of the water from the flowers down the front of my shirt when I picked them up. My hands trembled as I walked inside. The funeral director met me as I entered.

"May I help you?" she asked.

"Yes," I replied. "I have these flowers for the, uh, uh...little girl," I stammered.

"Right this way," she smiled, took the flowers, and turned in the opposite direction.

I followed her. My mouth was parched, and my breath came in short pants. I didn't realize she was taking me to the chapel. I saw the foot of the coffin. I stopped and shuddered. Let it be a closed casket, please, please, please.

Why was I torturing myself this way? I could have just mailed the letter, but I just had to bring myself here. Was I ignorant?

The tiny casket sat in the front of the room with the lid open. Inside was the body of a little girl the same age as our cousin Samantha. This little girl had blond hair, the same color as Andi's, and a small, rounded face. She was dressed in a beautiful flowing dress, and her little hands were neatly folded on her chest. I glanced at her for only a moment because, emotionally, I was not prepared to deal with the body of a murdered child. I noticed the bruising on her neck from being strangled, and my knees went a little weak. The resemblance to Andi was uncanny. She looked like a little sleeping angel. Softly in the background, I could hear an organ playing a sad tune. It was a surreal feeling. Seeing this child in that casket was not only wrong but also unnatural. I knew in my heart that this child had been robbed of her life. It wasn't her time to die. She had a full life ahead, and it had been stolen from her.

I cried the entire way home. The tears wouldn't stop. I pulled the car over for a few minutes to regain composure. My body ached. I went to bed when I got home. I was emotionally and physically drained.

A few months later, the child's aunt called me and told me the child's mother had received my letter and wanted to speak to me. She needed help, and she wasn't coping well. I called her and offered words of comfort and encouragement. We spoke several times over the next few months, and it was then she told me they had no support through the criminal justice system and asked if I would accompany them to court. I hesitated to think of my own horrific experience in the courtroom in Arkansas without a victim-witness coordinator. Hearing her voice quivering in pain, I told her I would go. This family needed support.

The preliminary hearing was held in October 2000. The family confided in me that they didn't know what was going to happen or why the prosecutor insisted they be there. I soon learned that the defense and the prosecution had come to an agreement. They had agreed on life without parole in exchange for no trial, where the child rapist and murderer most likely would have received the death penalty. The defense team thanked the prosecutor for this opportunity and stated that they themselves thought the facts of the case fit felony murder better, meaning a great possibility of the death penalty. This was all done without asking the child's family what they thought or wanted—the family wanted the death penalty for the monster who strangled their precious child. They wept as I explained to them what had just happened. The child's father was especially distraught. I took him by the hands and assured him that the killer would never hurt anyone again.

"I want him to pay for her murder; he's not going to pay."

"He's going to prison for the rest of his life, and he will never get out," I said.

"But he lived, she died. It's not fair."

"I know, I know. I am so sorry," I told him.

Then that six-foot-five man stood up and embraced me and wept like I've never heard anyone weep, it was more of a wail, really. I held him tight and let him cry. I thought he would never stop.

It was at this precise moment I decided that I would dedicate my life to fighting for all these little children who deserved justice. Images of that little angel lying in her casket with strangulation bruises on her neck were forever seared in my mind. Not fair, now or ever. I knew I had to fight for these little ones.

Just then, a Bible verse popped into my head: I heard a still, small voice saying, *'Whom shall I send, and who will go for us?'* *Then I said, 'Here am I. Send me.'* —Isaiah 6:8

God, this isn't what I want to do with my life. But here I am. I will go. Send me.

It was the first time I had talked to God in a long while.

APRIL 10, 2001

Coping had become slightly easier in the past year. Grief was such a bastard; however, I occupied myself by speaking to children, parents, and law enforcement about the importance of child safety— trying to go forward with life. I kept the child safety issue in the media whenever the chance arose. I also enrolled in the local community college to complete my basic requirements.

What would have been Andi's fourteenth birthday was a beautiful day. Mom, Kristy, and I headed to visit the grave. Several months before, I had begun to do some soul-searching and had decided it was time for me to go to the crime scene area. The prosecutor's office had also informed me that the trial transcripts were ready for me to pick up—twenty-five books, two inches deep each. I pondered the decision to read them and decided that the time had come. I would pick up the transcripts while I was there and read them when I got home. It wasn't reading about the trial that bothered me but reading the autopsy report from the crime lab and the written confession. But something inside me told me it was time.

Once at the cemetery, I peered at the immaculate grave. A ripple of thanksgiving swept through me. Ann Brewer, Andi's paternal grandmother, had promised that if we buried Andi in Arkansas, she would take care of the site. She didn't disappoint me. Andi's place of rest was beautiful. White rock outlined with brick, garnished with flowers, ceramic animals, cherubs, and wind chimes made it peaceful and comforting. I placed my hand on the faceplate—touched the rough surface of her name. Fourteen. She would have been fourteen. It didn't seem real. I took a breath, and my head began to throb. No matter how many days, weeks, months, or years passed, the pain was always there. More recently, I had been able to manage it better, to smile and laugh more. I found myself not feeling so guilty about living again. But times like these intensified the pain. Digging into my purse, I pulled out a bottle of Tylenol, shook a couple of pills into my hand, and swallowed them dry.

Ann, followed by several girls who had gone to school with Andi, pulled pink balloons from her car. Fourteen of them—representing the age she would have been. Releasing the balloons had become a ritual that Ann planned to perform each year, adding one balloon per year. In honor. In memory.

The grave tending and balloon release was her way to grieve. Ann had struggled with her own guilt. Karl had given her a final blow when he told his defense team he had killed Andi because of something Ann had said, something she had suggested. She was coping better, and taking care of the gravesite had helped her in a way. There was rarely a day she didn't visit. She told me people in town thought she was crazy. She said she didn't care; they had never lost a grandchild the way she had.

I recalled the past two years. Looking around at the small crowd gathering, I searched each face. They all had their own pain to deal with. Each of Andi's friends had tears running down their faces. My sister, Kristy, stood silently with a pink balloon whipping above her head. She was the quiet one. I knew she had struggled the past two years—losing Andi, going through a painful divorce, having her baby alone, an ex-husband who didn't care. Sadness. She had not been able to attend the trial; she was nine months pregnant. The closure of that chapter for her was still open, like a silent void. She felt like she had failed Andi by not attending. She loved Andi and had spent a lot of time with her. One movie they watched together was *Titanic*, and it turned out to be one of Andi's favorites. She particularly liked the *Heart of the Ocean* necklace. Kristy had a replica of the necklace. Andi had begged for the necklace, and Kristy would not give it to her because she had received it as a gift.

"Andi, when I die, you can have it."

She told me later how terrible she felt now about that comment.

"She died before me; she died before I could give it to her."

Kristy wiped her bangs out of her eyes and looked defeated, standing next to Andi's grave, waiting for Ann to signal the release of the balloons. I felt sorry for her and was sad that I had not been there for her.

I glanced at my mother. She had aged in the past two years. The aftermath of the crime had ripped her heart out. Thinking back to the week of the trial, one day after court, I had bought a rose to lay on Andi's grave and drove out to the cemetery to place it there. When I rounded the corner, I noticed Mom's red Ford pickup parked in front of the towering headstone. She had her face in her hands, sobbing. A flashback of when I saw her for the first time after the police told us Andi was dead hit me. Maybe she had not seen me; maybe I could turn around. My first reaction was to drive away, pretend I hadn't seen her, but I didn't. I pulled up behind her truck, placed my vehicle in park, and got out. She kept sobbing. In all my years, I had never seen my mother cry like that. I felt helpless and weak. She had always been a pillar, and it felt funny to see her weeping uncontrollably. I walked over to her. This time, I wanted to help her. Now, I would be strong for her and not push her away emotionally. Never again would I tell anyone that I couldn't handle their pain. How selfish of me. Seeing my mother cry stopped me from doing that. I took her in my arms and let her cry.

Snapping back to the balloon ceremony, my mother was now talking to Ann Brewer about the pretty wind chimes she had hung on the grave. Ann informed her that they would probably be stolen in the next week. Andi's grave ornaments were a favorite among local thieves. We couldn't stop people from stealing things. We had debated with law enforcement about putting surveillance video out and catching the culprit. Greg's brother, Jeff, had become extremely irate when things disappeared.

"The son-of-a-bitch will burn in hell for stealing from a little girl's grave," he would rant.

I agreed with him.

"Okay, we are ready to let them fly," Ann announced.

We let them go, and they soared. It was lovely.

"Happy Birthday, Andi," I whispered.

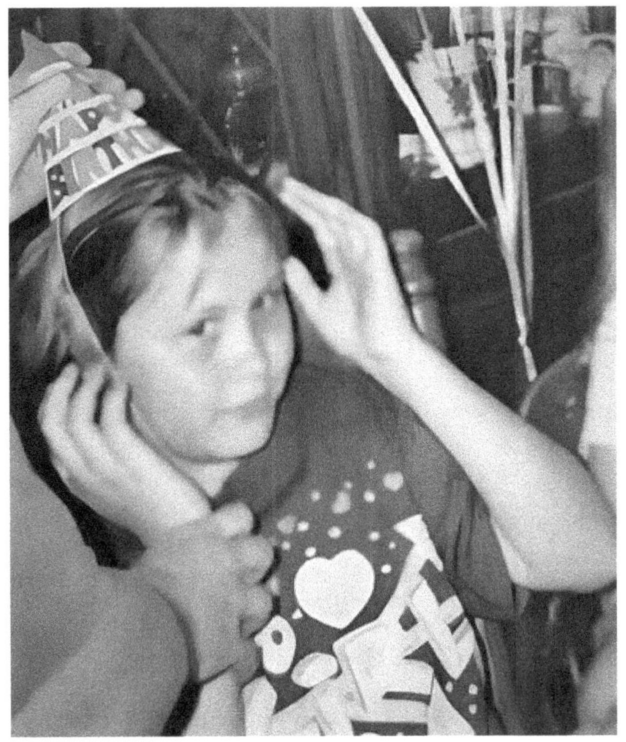

Deciding to visit the crime scene had been a two-year process for me. At first, I had no intention of ever going there. I didn't want to know—I didn't want the vision of that place in my mind. But something happened to me that spring when the need to know everything overwhelmed me. I wanted to drive the route Karl had taken with Andi. I wanted to see the place where he took and murdered her, and I wanted to read the autopsy report.

After releasing the balloons, I asked Mom and Kristy if they wanted to go. They said yes. Ann Brewer accompanied us.

The ride to Cove was made with nervous chatter. I was secretly haunted by the images in my mind as we drove.

What was she thinking when he took her? Did she fight him? Why didn't she jump out?

The countryside buzzed by, and I thought about how sad it was that the last thing she ever saw was the sky and the treetops as she lay on her back being raped—in utter terror. My poor little girl.

Looking forward, I saw Randall's grocery coming into view; we were in Cove. I clicked the right turn signal, and we turned at the grocery store. The county road was lined with houses, some quaint, some run-down, further on trees and then a chicken house. Following the curvy road for about a mile, we came to an old logging road.

"This is it," Ann said quietly.

I turned and pressed the gas slowly. The road was bumpy and filled with potholes and tree roots. To the side of the dirt road, litter lined the dense woods. I kept driving, and the road became narrow, like a tunnel. The huge trees provided a canopy that gave the illusion it was getting dark.

"How far back?" I asked Ann.

"A little ways."

We drove another quarter mile when Ann told me we were there.

It was a place where the road had a pull-off that jutted to the left. I knew this was where he had pulled off. In my mind:

"Take me home."

"Shut up."

"What are you going to do to me?"

"I am going to fuck you."

Hate washed over me and caused me to shudder. I wanted Karl to rot in hell. I wanted him to die.

Ann Brewer pointed to the ground. "That's where the bastard did it."

I glanced at the rock-hard ground.

"And he dragged her way back over there," she said, turning

and pointing in the opposite direction.

We walked to the place fifty yards away, and I wondered if the pile of brush lying close to the ground was the same brush he had used to cover her small nude body.

I had had enough. I turned and headed back to the truck, leaving the others standing there. I had a cross—a white one with Andi's name on it and yellow flowers—to stake in the ground. I needed a moment alone.

Opening the back hatch of my Dodge Durango, I saw the white cross lying in the back seat. I had brought a hammer to pound it into the ground. I picked them both up.

Was this what it had all boiled down to? Me traipsing through the woods, trying to find answers, trying to figure out why? There were no answers to be found here in the woods west of Cove, Arkansas. This couldn't bring Andi back, but at least I knew. At least I wouldn't be haunted by images of the unknown.

Picking up the cross, I walked to the place where Andi had died, raised the hammer, and hit the cross with all my might. Anger rose. I hit it again, and more anger was released. I hit it one last time, and the cross stood upright.

I stepped back to observe my handiwork:

Andi Brewer

4-10-87

5-15-99

Always Loved. Never Forgotten.

I got into the vehicle and waited for the others. I had faced the demon; I was finished here.

CHAPTER 21
EARLY MAY 2001

Twenty-five bound books of court documents were piled in front of me. I had picked them up in Mena before we left on Andi's birthday. I had moved them to my closet but had not had the nerve to look at them yet.

With the thickly bound volumes before me, I hesitated before picking one up and began to thumb through it. Most of it was jury selection and the trial; I had attended most of it, and it was repetitive to read over.

Then, I picked up the one labeled: **State Crime Laboratory, Report of Laboratory Analysis.**

I held it in my hands, then opened the first page and began.

I felt like I was reading the beginning of a horror novel.

POLYGRAPH:

FINDINGS

The physiological responses noted on this subject's polygraph charts are in such a pattern as to indicate that the subject, Karl D. Roberts, has not been completely truthful in answering the above questions.

Based on information furnished this examiner, interviews with the subject, and evaluation of the subject's polygraph charts; it is the opinion of this examiner that Karl D. Roberts has not been completely truthful.

Respectfully submitted,

Investigator Ocie Rateliff
Polygraph Examiner
Arkansas State Police
Company "C"

OWR/kgm

C: File #13-422-99
Inv. Ocie Rateliff

I realized the polygraph was not admissible in court, but this test had caused Karl Roberts to confess. I found it particularly interesting and heartbreaking at the same time. I continued to thumb through the booklet. There was so much paperwork from law enforcement. I wondered if they had ever stopped to think that one day, the victim's mother would be looking at this, reading it thoroughly. Probably not.

I realized I was not the "normal" victim. But I had always been one to push against the grain. That was why I felt it was important to share the full ugliness of this story. No candy coating; the truth needed to be told. The truth needed to be heard. The truth needed to be shown. Crime victims deserved to know the truth. No one needed to be led blindly down this path, and I wanted to help them as much as I could.

STATE CRIME LABORATORY
REPORT OF LABORATORY ANALYSIS:

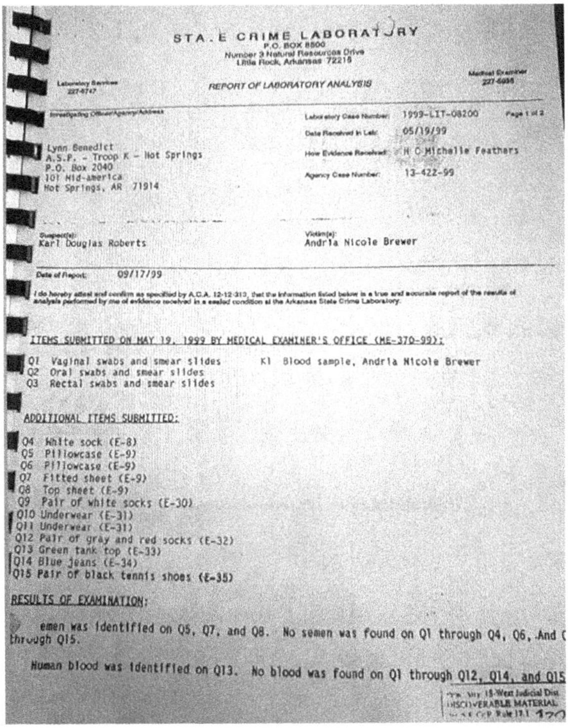

STA.E CRIME LABORATORY
P.O. BOX 8500
Number 3 Natural Resources Drive
Little Rock, Arkansas 72215

Laboratory Services
227-5747

REPORT OF LABORATORY ANALYSIS

Medical Examiner
227-5935

Investigating Officer/Agency/Address

Laboratory Case Number: 1999-LIT-08200   Page 1 of 2

Date Received In Lab: 05/19/99

Lynn Benedict
A.S.P. - Troop K - Hot Springs
P.O. Box 2040
101 Mid-america
Hot Springs, AR 71914

How Evidence Received: H O Michelle Feathers

Agency Case Number: 13-422-99

Suspect(s):
Karl Douglas Roberts

Victim(s):
Andria Nicole Brewer

Date of Report: 09/17/99

I do hereby attest and confirm as specified by A.C.A. 12-12-313, that the information listed below is a true and accurate report of the results of analysis performed by me of evidence received in a sealed condition at the Arkansas State Crime Laboratory.

ITEMS SUBMITTED ON MAY 19, 1999 BY MEDICAL EXAMINER'S OFFICE (ME-370-99):

Q1 Vaginal swabs and smear slides   K1 Blood sample, Andria Nicole Brewer
Q2 Oral swabs and smear slides
Q3 Rectal swabs and smear slides

ADDITIONAL ITEMS SUBMITTED:

Q4 White sock (E-8)
Q5 Pillowcase (E-9)
Q6 Pillowcase (E-9)
Q7 Fitted sheet (E-9)
Q8 Top sheet (E-9)
Q9 Pair of white socks (E-30)
Q10 Underwear (E-31)
Q11 Underwear (E-31)
Q12 Pair of gray and red socks (E-32)
Q13 Green tank top (E-33)
Q14 Blue jeans (E-34)
Q15 Pair of black tennis shoes (E-35)

RESULTS OF EXAMINATION:

emen was identified on Q5, Q7, and Q8. No semen was found on Q1 through Q4, Q6, And Q
through Q15.

Human blood was identified on Q13. No blood was found on Q1 through Q12, Q14, and Q15

15-West Judicial Dist
DISCOVERABLE MATERIAL
A.R.CrP. Rule 17.1 170

Vaginal swabs.

Rectal swabs.

Smear slides.

Blood sample.

Human blood.

Bile rose in my throat. Burning. Why was I doing this to myself? I wanted to know the details, but I didn't want to know. I read on. I was so devastated, and it hurt so deeply. My mind slowly opened a door I wished it had never opened, but I had gone too far to stop.

I was in a scary dream where you saw a hand reach for a doorknob. A hand—my hand—reached out, and before I could grasp the knob, the door opened before I touched it to reveal the most hideous monster one could ever imagine.

Death stared at me, and it looked like this: the autopsy of my girl. My Andit Bandit. There was no need to hide the truth because, so many times, the truth was candy-coated. I wanted the truth and nothing but the truth to be known because this crime was ugly. This crime was heinous.

I knew this was something the anti-death penalty lobby didn't want to be exposed, so I had chosen to share it. This was what the anti-death penalty machine tried to hide.

And one line that jumped out most to me was, "cratered animal feeding marks" and "fly eggs and first-stage larvae," but "the tip of the tongue was clenched in the teeth."

She had nearly bit her tongue off, fighting for her life. Oh my god!

Name: BREWER, And... N.   Date: 05/18/99

EXTERNAL EXAMINATION

The body was that of an unclad, normally developed and normally nourished adolescent white female. Decompositional changes were present and will be further described below. Bags were present on the hands at initial examination. Initial examination revealed the upper legs to be abducted at approximately a 45 degree angle, with the lower legs slightly flexed at the knees. The body weighed 121 pounds and was 60 inches in height. The overall appearance of the body was consistent with the reported age of 12 years. The body was cool. Rigor was waning in all extremities. Lividity was present and fixed on the posterior surface of the body except in areas exposed to pressure and areas where obscured by postmortem changes. Decompositional changes and other postmortem changes include facial bloating and green-black discoloration with the presence of fly eggs and first stage larvae, protuberance of the eyes with green-red postmortem discoloration of the sclerae and conjunctival surfaces with opaqueness of the cornea, sloughing of the hair, areas of epidermal blistering on the anterior neck, with green-black discoloration of the anterior neck and upper chest, marbling of the anterior aspects of the arms, moderate abdominal bloating with truncal subcutaneous air collection, green discoloration of the back of the scalp, green-black discoloration of the back of the upper neck and back, red and green discoloration with marbling of the right back and buttocks, skin slippage of the buttocks, and multiple yellow-brown superficial and cratered animal feeding marks on the posterior aspect of the legs. There was dirt and vegetable debris adherent to the posterior aspects of the body and the upper extremities. The scalp hair was brown. The irides were red-brown, with decompositional discoloration. The corneae were cloudy. There was red-brown purge fluid in the nasal cavities. Bloating of the lips was present. The tip of the tongue was clenched in the teeth. The teeth were natural and in good dental condition. The external auditory canals were dry. Examination of the neck revealed the postmortem changes as described above. There was generalized glistening and moist decompositional changes of the epidermis, with moderate postmortem swelling. The chest appeared to be symmetrically developed. Initial first stage breast development was noted. Several hairs were present on the abdomen and collected. The female genitalia were of normal developmental stage for the reported age. Scant pubic hair was present. Other genital changes will be described below. The legs showed apparent normal development. The upper extremities were normally developed with no tattoos or wrist scars noted. The spine was palpably intact. The anus showed postmortem mucosal prominence, no external evidence of injury was noted. There was focal fecal incontinence and some coarse hair around the perineal area, which was collected. The posterior surface of the body showed normal development.

EVIDENCE OF MEDICAL ATTENTION:

None.

7 Page Report/Page 2

CHAPTER 22

The phone rang. It was Colleen Nick. She didn't know what I had just read, what I had learned about Andi's final moments on earth—that she had nearly bitten her tongue in half.

"Rebecca, are you sitting down?"

"Yes," I answered.

"The Department of Justice wants you to speak at the Missing Children's ceremony in Washington, DC. They want you to represent the nation's missing children this year."

"Me?"

"Yes, you, and here's the kicker. You will be speaking on the platform with Attorney General Ashcroft. Will you do it?"

"Of course, I will do it. Remember, it was you who told me that I was Andi's voice." I smiled weakly, glancing at the documents.

"Yes, you are."

I didn't tell her I was staring at a mountain of court documents. I didn't tell her at all that I had decided to face my fears, my nightmares, my horrific visions. I was going to confront them all before I stood in the nation's capital, before I did any more advocacy work at all.

We made small talk and finally hung up. I looked back at the records and sat down on the floor again.

"The body was that of an unclad, normally developed, normally nourished adolescent white female. Decompositional changes were present. The body was cool. Rigor mortis was waning in all extremities. Lividity was present and fixed on the posterior surface of the body except in areas exposed to pressure and where obscured by postmortem changes."

I skipped down a little, and the part about her tongue caught my eye.

"The tip of the tongue was clenched in the teeth."

My stomach churned.

She bit her tongue.

I couldn't get past that part. She bit her tongue!

I dropped the book and ran to the bathroom. My knees hit the floor; pain shot up my legs. I grabbed the toilet and heaved. Nothing came up. I was so sick of the feeling of having to throw up and not being able to do it.

He choked her, and she bit her tongue before she died. She had been fighting—fighting for her little life.

Cruel and depraved.

I sat back. My mind reeled. That son-of-a-bitch.

I began to sob. I needed someone to listen. I couldn't talk to Kris. He couldn't talk about it. He seemed to avoid me more these days.

Colleen answered on the first ring.

"She bit her tongue nearly in half before she died."

"What?"

"She bit her tongue hard before she died. I read the autopsy report, and she bit the tip of her tongue," I sobbed, the words coming in short gulps of air.

Colleen began to cry with me; she knew that sometimes, not saying anything at all was best.

CHAPTER 23
NATIONAL MISSING CHILDREN'S DAY
WASHINGTON DC
MAY 25, 2001

I was trying my best to cope with all this—the new life that had been thrust upon me. I occupied myself by speaking to children, parents, and law enforcement about the importance of child safety—trying to move forward with life. I worked hard to keep the child safety issue in the media whenever the chance arose. I was also determined to finish college. I had a deep-rooted desire to attain my bachelor's degree. This, along with family life, kept my mind from dwelling on what had happened. I had to stay busy.

It was early May when I received the official call from the Department of Justice asking if I was interested in being a speaker for the Missing Children's Day ceremony in Washington, DC. I said yes.

The morning was splendid. The rays of sunlight made the

Washington Monument stark white. I felt so out of place, like I didn't belong with this caliber of people. All these important people, all these suits. I was expected to take the podium at 2:00 and tell Andi's story in the Robert F. Kennedy Department of Justice Building in the Great Hall. The speech I intended to give never left my right jacket pocket. The entire morning, I checked it continuously to make sure it was there. Without that prepared speech, I knew I would just stare, awestruck, at the crowd of dignitaries I knew would be there.

But first, a Congressional breakfast. I was with two other mothers who had missing children—Colleen, mother of Morgan, and Patty Wetterling, mother of Jacob. They led me to a table, and we sat down to a feast of breakfast food. Bacon, eggs, sausage, all the fruit one could imagine, biscuits, gravy, and a table setting fit for a king. I didn't even know which fork to use first, so I watched everyone. However, I couldn't eat much, knowing I had to speak to such a large crowd later, so I picked at a bagel and nibbled a piece of bacon.

After breakfast, awards were presented to law enforcement officers for bringing home missing children and protecting them from predatory crime. Several children were awarded for their bravery in escaping from a child abductor.

Next, John Walsh took the podium and gave a moving speech about his son, Adam, who had been kidnapped and murdered, and the things that were being accomplished on his television show, *America's Most Wanted.* Actress Jamie Lee Curtis followed, kicking off a national child safety program.

After breakfast, Colleen grabbed my elbow and pulled me through the crowd. Patty followed close behind us.

"I want to introduce you to John Walsh," Colleen said.

The three of us weaved our way to where Walsh was being flocked by fans. He spotted us and waved us over.

"Hi, Colleen. Hi, Patty. It's so good to see you both."

He had covered Morgan and Jacob's stories several times on his show. They hugged him, and Colleen introduced me.

"This is Rebecca. Her 12-year-old daughter, Andi, was kidnapped and murdered a few years ago," she told him.

"I am so sorry," he said and gave me a hug. "You know she is looking at you from heaven and watching out for you; she is your angel."

I nodded.

"She's beautiful," he said, touching the button pinned to my lapel with Andi's photo on it.

"Thank you."

"Rebecca is the keynote speaker today at the ceremony with the Attorney General," Colleen told him.

"That's great," Walsh replied. "You keep up the good work. Never stop fighting for your daughter." He looked deep into my eyes. "Never. Stop."

"I won't, I promise," I said.

After visiting with John Walsh, I noticed that Bryan Cranston, the *Malcolm in the Middle* dad (years later, a very popular blue meth-cooking dad named Walter White on the hit show *Breaking Bad*), was in attendance promoting child safety as well. We made small talk, and he asked how I became involved with the issue of promoting child safety. I told him Andi's story, and he hugged me, his eyes filling with tears. Then, we posed for a picture. It was all very surreal.

Leaving the Congressional breakfast, we hopped into a cab and headed over to the National Center for Missing and Exploited Children headquarters in Alexandria, Virginia. John Walsh's producer stepped off the elevator and told us that Jamie Lee Curtis was waiting upstairs for us in a private room. Colleen, Patty, and I stepped into the elevator.

Jamie Lee Curtis. Waiting for us?

We exited the elevator and walked down the hall. We entered the room, and there she was—more beautiful than she was in the movies—tall, slender, and eloquent. She greeted us, shook our hands, and began small talk. Her producer interrupted to tell her she had thirty minutes before production time. Jamie Lee thanked her. We had thirty minutes alone with Jamie Lee Curtis. Andi had loved her in the movie *My Girl.*

"Rebecca," she said gently, her blue eyes sparkling. "Tell me about your daughter, the reason you are here today."

For the next twenty minutes, I relayed Andi's story. She held her hand over her mouth in shock. When I finished, she touched the button on my lapel.

"She's very lovely."

With tears in her eyes, she pulled me into her arms and kissed the top of my head. She smelled like sweet lilacs.

"God bless you. I am so sorry." She kept me in her arms for what seemed like an eternity and patted my back. In awe of her stardom, I could only think, *Wow, I am being embraced by Jamie Lee Curtis. This is Jamie Lee Curtis, and she knows about my Andi.*

I felt a sense of pride, not in meeting all these people, but in knowing that Andi would not be forgotten. Jamie Lee talked to Colleen and Patty as they relayed their heartbreaking stories. Our thirty minutes turned into an hour. Then, we posed for photos and hugged goodbye.

HALL OF JUSTICE
WASHINGTON, DC
2:00 PM

Though it was pre-September 11, 2001, the security was tight. We went through a metal detector at the door and an identification check. I walked down the large corridor toward the Great Hall of Justice. When I walked into the room, my eyes grew large as the Great Hall opened before me. A glamorous two-story room the department used for special occasions was graced by two statues looming elevated on the platform. The sculptures, two art deco aluminum statues, were placed in the building in 1930 when the building was completed. The female Spirit of Justice held her arms high. The toga she wore covered one breast. The male, Majesty of Justice, stood strong and sure, a loin cloth covering his mid-section.

Standing there in awe, Colleen gently touched my elbow.

"I have to take you to the front and introduce you to the people who arranged this speaking engagement for you."

"Okay," I replied.

She led me to the front of the platform. Approaching the three men in front, they paused when we reached them.

"Rebecca, this is Ernie Allen, President of the National Center for Missing and Exploited Children, and Ron Laney, head of the Offices of Juvenile Justice and Delinquency Program, here at the Department of Justice."

"My pleasure," I said, shaking hands with each.

"You will be coming backstage with me, Rebecca," Allen said. "The ceremony will be starting soon. The Attorney General should arrive at any moment. We will want to be backstage waiting for him."

Before walking up on the platform and slipping backstage, I glanced behind me. About two hundred people had already filed in and were looking for a seat. I fought the urge to chew my nails.

I waited with Ernie Allen, who made small talk with me, asking where I was from and how I had been doing. It was then that I noticed Allen move his head to the left to peer behind me.

"There's the Attorney General," Allen said.

Waltzing backstage from an undisclosed door, Attorney General Ashcroft stepped up to us and introduced himself.

"This is Rebecca, the parent representative of the nation's missing children this year. She lost her daughter Andi to abduction and murder."

"I'm so very sorry you lost your daughter," he said politely. "Looks like today you will get to speak on her behalf."

"Yes, sir," was all I could say.

"Time to go out," someone yelled from behind us.

"Rebecca, you will be the last speaker," Mr. Allen said.

"Okay," my voice quivered.

I could not believe that I was on the stage with the Attorney General of the United States, representing the missing children of this nation. I was nobody, just a suburban housewife.

I led the way onto the stage and walked across the platform to the opposite side where our chairs were placed. Sitting down in the far-left seat, I peered out at the large crowd.

There must be three hundred people here.

My hands started to sweat.

The ceremony began with some more awards being given to law enforcement.

Then Attorney General Ashcroft spoke, assuring those in attendance of the government's commitment to the safety of children. Next, he gave an award to a child who had designed a drawing relating to the issue of missing children.

After he finished, the master of ceremonies introduced me.

"Three years ago, our next guest lost her young daughter, Andi, to abduction and murder. Now a mother on a mission, she has spoken to law enforcement, parents, children, and communities on the issues of child safety. She has a powerful voice and is joining us today to share her story."

I stood up, my heart jumping, and walked to the podium, pausing for a moment to scan the crowd. Locating Colleen in the midsection to my right, I made eye contact with her and began to speak. Honored to be chosen to represent the nation's missing children, I gave this opportunity my best shot. I told Andi's story—how she was a beautiful child who wanted to teach, loved children and animals.

"Andi didn't deserve the crime that befell her. No child deserves to be the victim of a predatory crime. No child deserves to be kidnapped and brutally murdered. I make a challenge to all of you here today to fight for the children of this nation. There is no number greater than zero when it comes to missing children."

I finished by thanking the Department of Justice and the National Center for Missing and Exploited Children for their efforts. I then thanked Andi.

"Andi, I know you are not here today in body, but you are here in spirit. I want to say to you thank you for teaching me about life—how to live, love, laugh, and grieve. Thank you for teaching me how to face the unimaginable and smile in the face of adversity. Thank you."

I turned and walked back toward my seat. The crowd exploded into applause and stood to their feet. I was the only one who received a standing ovation. Attorney General Ashcroft hugged me.

"I am proud of what you are doing—I am proud to call you a fellow American citizen. You have a powerful testimony. Keep it alive. Never stop what you are doing."

"Thank you, Mr. Ashcroft."

The Bells of Love took center stage next, a child-singing group created in the memory of abducted, murdered child Sara Wood. Their beautiful voices filled the Great Hall. They sang a song called *Light the Way Home* and dedicated it to me, Colleen, Patty, and John Walsh—for all the wonderful things we had done. I was touched by their kindness and was emotionally moved when a small blonde-haired girl placed a bouquet of flowers in my arms.

"This is for you," she said sweetly. "Thank you for keeping kids like me safe."

Tears again.

CHAPTER 24
THE EIGHT-YEAR-OLD CHAMPION

That evening, with the weight of the world off my shoulders, several of us decided to go sightseeing. Personally, I wanted to ride the Metro (I had never been on the Metro or the subway) and see the White House up close, experience the Washington Monument, and visit the Lincoln Memorial. Just being in the nation's Capitol was a treat. Never having gone too far from Arkansas and Oklahoma, all these things intrigued me because I never thought I would ever have a reason to see them at all. Life had changed on a whim, and now, here I was. It was an awesome experience, especially now that I didn't have to keep up with that speech in my right jacket pocket.

While waiting on the Metro station platform, I noticed a little girl. Brown teardrop eyes, the color of a Hershey's Kiss, with shoulder-length bobbed brown hair. I realized it was the child who had won the award for being the "Bravest Child in the Nation" at the ceremony where I had spoken in the Great Hall. She locked eyes with me, and a smile spread across her face. I smiled back at her. This little 8-year-old girl had survived a horror story that no child should ever experience. She had been kidnapped while walking home from school several months earlier; it was her 8th birthday. Her brother, trotting closely behind, witnessed her being pulled violently into a car. It was later found that the man who had kidnapped her had already abducted and murdered two other young girls.

After the initial abduction in front of her brother, this man had kept this child shackled in his vehicle for two days and repeatedly sexually assaulted her. A few times, he had left her alone, shackled by the legs in the floorboard of his vehicle, while he went inside and watched her mother crying for her return on the nightly news.

With the mind of an adult, this little girl, even during her nightmare, had found a nail file in the floorboard of the car and picked at the ankle lock. All hope had seemed to disappear when it broke. Finally, the predator made the mistake of leaving his keys in the car while he ran into the store. At this point, she grabbed them from the ignition and, using the smallest key on the ring first, she unlocked her shackles.

In the nick of time, she leaped from the vehicle as the perpetrator exited the store. She dashed across the parking lot to a parked semi-truck and scurried up the side and into the open window, landing in the lap of the stunned trucker.

"I'm the girl who was kidnapped," she screamed. "That man pulling his car out of the parking lot is the one who took me," she pointed.

The truck driver, in haste, quickly wrote down the tag number, and within hours, the perpetrator was arrested. He was convicted of a life sentence for kidnapping, rape, and the murder of another child. He had since died in prison from complications due to kidney failure. Death had gotten him in the end, I supposed. Death would always get them in the end.

However, on this day, she recognized me from the speech I had given in the Great Hall. I saw her asking her mother if she could come over to talk to me, and since we were taking the same Metro train into the city, she said yes. This little, brown-eyed girl ran over to me.

"I heard your speech today," she said, slightly out of breath. "I think it was wonderful." She was extremely bright for her age. Of course, she had escaped a killer.

"Thank you." I wanted to hug her, but I refrained. I didn't know if she was okay with that; it had only been a few months since her escape.

"May I sit by you on the Metro?" she asked, her brown eyes piercing my heart.

"Of course, you can if it's okay with your mom and dad."

"Mom, can I sit by her? Please?"

Her mother smiled and nodded.

I gladly welcomed her. We made small talk about the sights in DC and about her school. Then she became very quiet, and I could see her eyes starting to close. The lull of the clicking tracks made me want to close my eyes too, but I didn't. When her eyes fell shut, I stared at her perfect sleeping face, examined her tiny features—little nose, perfect lips, rosy cheeks—and prayed that she would keep fighting and grow up to be a warrior. Not a victim who gave up. But a champion gladiator. I wondered if she realized she was very lucky to be alive. I felt very blessed to be sitting next to her at all. Statistically speaking, she should have been in some lone cemetery. But she had fought the beast and won.

*Click, click, click...*the tracks lulled.

I wondered how she had done it, how she had kept her spirit fighting enough to survive and get away; she couldn't have weighed more than maybe sixty pounds. I cringed at the thought of having to fight that monster. The nightmare she had survived seemed very close to home. It made me wonder why Andi had not run for her life—or had she? Maybe there just wasn't enough time to plot her escape. Why hadn't she jumped from the vehicle? Had I taught her to be too nice? To respect her elders? I wished I knew.

I glanced down again at this sleeping angel, breathing so softly and peacefully. I felt sick that there were people in the world who had a desire to rape and hurt children. It was then I realized that if you didn't know the story behind what had happened to this little girl months before, you would never know what she had lived through, what she had fought through. She showed no outward signs of the horrifying ordeal. She rested peacefully as though nothing had happened. A child who had been drawn to me, one who had a desire to be seated next to me—the mother of a little girl who had not made it home alive. It was like a salve to my heart. She had heard and had been comforted by *my* words. I was comforted by her very living existence. It seemed that, in her childlike way, she was telling me that everything was going to be okay. That sometimes, children did make it home alive.

I would never forget the lesson she had taught me.

And I had to hold onto that lesson because what happened next was something the news media dubbed "The Year of Abductions." It shook and terrified our nation. The highest leaders of our country knew something had to be done. It was something the state of Texas and a handful of other states called the **Amber Alert.**

CHAPTER 25
THE NATIONAL AMBER ALERT
SEPTEMBER 2002

Who hangs up on the White House? Apparently, me.

It was a normal day with normal routine activities. I was sitting on my bedroom floor, folding towels and watching television. The phone rang. When I picked up, a woman said, "Please hold for an important call from the White House."

I figured it was a telemarketer wanting to rattle off their sales pitch for some junk I didn't need. Only one way to get rid of them.

Click.

The phone immediately rang again. I almost didn't answer, thinking it was probably more of the same. But after a few rings, I couldn't resist and picked up again.

It was a real person on the line—a woman.

"We must have lost connection. I have an important call for

you from the White House."

I was still skeptical. The White House? It couldn't be real...or could it?

Intrigued, I tossed the towel back into the basket and listened as the woman invited me to a panel discussion on Missing, Exploited, and Runaway Children in Washington, D.C. According to her, the White House was hosting a conference, and the President was expected to speak.

As my brain started to absorb the information, I couldn't help but ask, "Pardon me, Ma'am, but why are you calling me? How do you even know about me?"

"You were the keynote speaker at National Missing Children's Day with Attorney General Ashcroft, right?"

"Yes."

"Well, you must have impressed someone at the Department of Justice."

"Really? Who?"

I could hear the smiling tone in her voice.

"Now, Ma'am. You know I can't tell you that."

"Sure, you can!" I blurted. "I won't tell anyone you told me!"

This time, she laughed outright. "I'm very sorry. I can't."

I only had a day to recover from my shock at this invitation before another call came with a change of plans. This time, they told me that I was being removed from the panel discussion. Instead, I would be taking part in a private roundtable discussion with ten other victim family members.

I immediately felt somewhat offended because the victim families were being pushed to the back burner. Before I could voice any objections, she began talking about what would be expected of me when the President entered the room, when the President approached me. When the President asked me questions, her quick eastern accent played on and on with such instructions until I couldn't help but speak up.

"Excuse me," I said, "I don't mean to interrupt...but the President of what?"

"The President of the United States, Ma'am."

"George Walker Bush?"

"Yes, ma'am. George Walker Bush."

Holy smokes.

"How did he get my number?"

There was a noticeable pause on the other end of the phone. And then the woman started laughing again.

My body trembled, and my hands were drenched with sweat as the Secret Service quickly entered the room and announced that President Bush was in the elevator on his way up.

"Address him as Mr. President and don't be nervous, he's a normal everyday guy," the Secret Service informed us.

"Only the leader of the free world," I whispered to the Federal Prosecutor on my left. She smiled, but I noticed she was wringing her hands.

Ten of us stood around a U-shaped table, waiting for him to enter. Tension hung heavily in the room, and I breathed in short puffs. My heart pounded in my chest. I could hear the swooshing sound in my ears. It wasn't as though I was waiting in line to get a quick glimpse of our nation's leader. I had been invited to join him at a private roundtable discussion. He wanted to hear my story; he wanted to hear Andi's story—he wanted to know what could be done to prevent this from happening to other children.

He entered the room with confidence and poise, the First Lady at his side. He made eye contact with me as I introduced myself. He clasped my hand firmly and shook it gently. I noticed that his hands were rough. *A hard-working man,* I thought, envisioning him on his ranch in Texas, working cattle. He made his way around the room, shaking hands with the others, and finally took his seat at the head of the table. Mrs. Bush sat to his right, and Margaret Spelling was on his left while the Secret Service agents positioned themselves in all four corners of the room.

"We take this issue very seriously because it's a national problem," the President stated, pausing slightly to make eye contact with each of us. "I'm a crier. I see tears in your eyes, so it makes me want to weep with you."

Wasting no time, he looked to his left. "Colleen, we will start with you."

Quoting First Corinthians, *"love always hopes,"* she proceeded to tell him of the 1995 abduction of her 6-year-old daughter, Morgan Nick, from a ballpark. She choked back tears as she recounted how Morgan, who had never been returned, was kidnapped by a stranger on that warm June night. She told him Morgan had wanted to be a doctor and a clown. She finished by stating that there needed to be a national Amber Alert so other children who were kidnapped could come home to the families who loved them.

Tears filled the President's eyes. "God bless you," he said.

Sharon Brooks spoke briefly, followed by her daughter, Tamara, who had been kidnapped in August with her friend, Jacqueline Marris, from a popular teen hangout. After the 12-hour-long ordeal, the girls were rescued by the police. The abductor was shot and killed. The Amber Alert had been used to aid in their rescue.

"Tamara, how old are you?" the President asked.

"Sixteen," she replied, smiling. She proceeded by telling him the gripping tale of her abduction. She described how she and Jackie had been restrained with duct tape and how the abductor did "some bad things" to them.

"He tried to make us drink whiskey, but we spit it out."

"Smart," Bush replied.

She went on to describe their failed escape attempt and how

she and her friend had stabbed their captor. She ended with the rescue, explaining how law enforcement had shot and killed the man responsible for taking them.

"Is there anything else you would like to add?" the President asked.

"Yes, never give up hope and live life to the fullest," Tamara finished.

He moved on to Kim Swartz of Vallejo, California. She told the story of her daughter, Amber, who had been kidnapped and never returned. Although her daughter was not the *Amber* of the famed Amber Alert, Swartz fully supported it and recommended placing tracking devices on sex offenders.

The Chavez family of Abilene, Texas, was next.

"My old stomping ground, West Texas," the President said.

Mr. Chavez quoted the Lord's Prayer and began to weep. Their infant daughter, Nancy, had been kidnapped from a Wal-Mart parking lot by a man who stole their minivan. Mrs. Chavez had been caught on the store's surveillance video screaming and hanging onto the door of the vehicle as it drove away with little Nancy. She fell off a few hundred yards later. The baby was found and returned to them after the Amber Alert was broadcast, leading to her rescue.

Michael Carona spoke next.

"I feel very inadequate being in this room today, and I won't take much time. I am here to say that I want the Amber Alert to be signed into national law."

Carona, the gutsy Orange County, California Sheriff, had quickly jumped into action when 5-year-old Samantha Runnion was kidnapped from Stanton, California. A man had approached and asked her and her friend to help him find his missing dog. He had then snatched Samantha, kicking and screaming. *"Help me! Tell my grandmother!"* she had yelled as he pulled her into the car. A massive search had ensued, and Carona hadn't wasted a moment. He quickly initiated the Amber Alert and used the power of the media to help find Samantha by putting out information about her abductor. Less than 24 hours later, two hang gliders had spotted the child's body discarded alongside a rural highway in Riverside County.

"Don't eat. Don't sleep. Because we're coming after you. We will take every resource that's available to us to bring you to justice," Carona had said in a media interview.

Because of the intense efforts, Samantha's abductor had been captured and was awaiting trial. The President informed Carona he was going to announce the expansion of the National Amber Alert that day.

Next, a mother whose child had been abducted overseas spoke about international abduction, followed by Federal Prosecutor Janis Gordon from Atlanta, who was seated next to me. She informed the President how she had gotten 15 pimps convicted for child prostitution rings and told him how the same thing could be done in other cities. She urged him to bring it to the attention of Attorney General John Ashcroft. Bush scribbled notes as she spoke and replied with, "I'm proud to call you an employee of the federal government."

The President looked at me. My stomach tightened and lurched.

"Rebecca, let's hear your story."

I could barely breathe. I kept my trembling hands under the table.

"Mr. President, thank you for inviting me here today to share my daughter Andi's story. It is such an honor, again, thank you." I bit my bottom lip for a moment to keep the tears from slipping down my face. My voice quivered as I continued, and I saw the President's eyes mist over. Mrs. Bush placed her hand on top of his.

"On May 15, 1999, my daughter was kidnapped from her rural Arkansas home. After a three-day statewide search, the abductor confessed to the FBI that he had taken her from her living room, driven her to a nearby town, down an old logging road, where he raped and strangled her to death. He covered her body with a scrub brush and later returned to assist with the search. My family has been devastated since that day. We loved her so much; she had great potential, but her life was stolen from her by a predator. Of course, no one knows for sure, but I believe in my heart that she could have possibly been saved by the Amber Alert. If someone had seen him driving her away and had heard that alert, they could have stopped this from happening, but that wasn't the case. She didn't have that chance and lost her life. So, I will finish by saying if there is one thing I could ask for from your administration, it would be for the National Amber Alert to be signed into federal law."

"God bless you," the President said comfortingly, wiping tears away.

After I finished, I realized that my hands had stopped shaking, and I felt peaceful, like Andi was watching from heaven, saying, *"I'm so proud of you, Mommy. Go, Mom, go."*

President Bush approached me, hugged me, and kissed my cheek. He autographed a picture for my youngest daughter, Kristin, and we posed for a photograph. I keep that photograph on my wall, and every time I look at it, I remember that day—as if I could forget. It was the day I shared Andi's story with the President of the United States of America. One of the most incredible days of my life.

A day I would gladly give up to spend one more moment with Andi.

APRIL 30, 2003

Over the next few months, I made several trips to DC regarding child advocacy work, but two stood out the most. The most exciting part was when I met President Bush. But I must mention another occasion that greatly affected me—my trip to the White House Rose Garden when President Bush signed the Child PROTECT Act of 2003—which, among other things, enabled the Amber Alert to be enacted immediately upon a child abduction. The bill also provided many other important tools to prevent, investigate, and prosecute violent crimes against children.

My daughter, Melanie, accompanied me on this trip. Our first stop was the Washington Press Club, where The National Center for Missing and Exploited Children and John Walsh introduced their new campaign to fight the sexual exploitation of children.

Cameras lined the back of the room as reporters awaited the

announcement of the new program: "America's Dirty Little Secret," which referred to the problem that occurred daily—the sexual exploitation and trafficking of children.

Nearby was a table spread with an assortment of finger foods: sandwiches, chips, fresh vegetables, and fruit. Melanie and I spotted it and made a beeline for it. Melanie grabbed some chips. The sandwiches looked great, but I was very self-conscious about getting food stuck in my teeth, so I chose fruit instead. I placed three slices of pineapple on my plate and grabbed a fork. I turned and scanned the crowd, holding my plate in front of me, trying to look as poised as possible.

But, when I tried to slice into the middle pineapple piece with my fork, the other two slices shot off my plate like cannonballs, landing a few feet on either side of me. Melanie was the only one who saw it; she grabbed her mouth to stifle a giggle.

"Shh!" I whispered, horrified, and picked up the fallen pineapple. I decided I should have had a sandwich instead.

Melanie couldn't look at me the rest of the day without laughing. Life was still worth living. I had two daughters who deserved to have a mother. Melanie's giggle warmed my heart. I hadn't heard it in a long while.

Later, while waiting outside to go into the gate of the White House, we visited with John Walsh, host of *America's Most Wanted*. I had not seen him since I met him at the Congressional breakfast a couple of years back. It was nice to see him and extra nice to be able to introduce him to Melanie. She was star-struck.

I knew he never really wanted the limelight, just to bring justice to his son, Adam, who had been kidnapped from Sears in 1981. We talked until the line began to move.

After going through a maze of security and the main corridor of the White House, we were led into the First Lady's Garden and told to wait for a short time while they prepared the Rose Garden for our arrival. There were several child advocates I knew from my travels, and we paused to take a few photographs. Melanie then stepped away to mingle with other siblings who had experienced the devastation of abduction.

Suddenly, I found myself alone. I gazed out at the Washington Monument from the White House lawn—a viewpoint I had never had before and might never have again. At that moment, I felt the urge to leave my footprints in this place. I glanced around to make sure no one was watching and slipped off my shoes.

When I was a kid, I used to run across the lawns in my neighborhood, loving the feel of thick Bermuda under the soles of my feet. That Bermuda, however, was nothing compared to what I stood on now. I felt my feet sinking into the most lush, soft emerald carpet I could ever have imagined. My toes disappeared as I dug them even deeper, trying to feel the dirt beneath the grass.

I could feel the Secret Servicemen's eyes on me. They made no move to stop me, though, and so I stood for a moment, absorbing my country's history from the ground up. I could almost hear the voices from the past whispering to me from the grass.

I felt as though I was in a bubble, with everyone bustling around me, talking, laughing, and mingling. Didn't they realize where they were standing? Didn't they stop to think about the people who had walked on this piece of earth, this historical sacred ground? Founding fathers, presidents, first ladies, dignitaries—their feet had graced the spot on which I stood.

Perhaps they did not... but I was not going to ignore the importance of this moment or this place where I was privileged to stand. I took it all in, every second. And I took deep, cleansing breaths.

I didn't slip my shoes back on until they called us into the Rose Garden. A handsome Marine Corps officer escorted us to our seats. I looked around, expecting to see masses of roses. Instead, I saw a mass of reporters and television cameras.

After we took our seats, children who had been rescued because of the activation of the Amber Alert were brought onto the lawn along with their families. Elizabeth Smart, the abducted and recovered teen from Salt Lake City, Utah, was also with this crowd, along with Tamara Brooks, who had been with me at the Round Table discussion months before. Finally, and most importantly, Donna Norris, mother of Amber Hagerman, for whom the Amber Alert was named, stood among them.

Attorney General Ashcroft and President Bush appeared and stood behind the podium. We all stood up and clapped. Each man gave a short speech, and then President Bush stepped aside and sat at a small desk. The children formed a semi-circle behind him.

The President made eye contact with Hagerman's mother. "Are you okay?" he asked.

"Yes," she said.

He nodded and signed the PROTECT Act of 2003—the most important bill that had ever been signed for missing, runaway, abducted, and exploited children. I took Melanie by the hand, and we both cried.

WASHINGTON DC
OCTOBER 3, 2002

Bush Unveils Upgrade of Amber Alert System
By ELISABETH BUMILLER
Published: October 3, 2002

President Bush listened with tears in his eyes today to wrenching stories from the parents of missing or murdered children, then announced that the federal government would spend $10 million to improve the Amber Alert systems set up to notify the public about abducted youths.

Mr. Bush also said that the Justice Department would name a new Amber Alert coordinator, and that it would develop a national standard for Amber systems – which include broadcasting messages on television and radio stations and posting information on electronic freeway signs – to try to accelerate the dissemination of alerts.

''The kidnapping of every child is a parent's worst nightmare,'' Mr. Bush said at a White House conference on missing, exploited and runaway children, with a large backdrop of photographs of missing children behind him. ''Yet too many moms and dads have experienced this nightmare across America.''

Mr. Bush added that he and his wife, Laura, had just met with parents ''who have had the most precious person in their lives suddenly and brutally taken away from them.''

Those parents included Rebecca (DeMauro) Petty of Oklahoma, whose 12-year-old daughter, Andria, was abducted, raped and murdered by an uncle in Arkansas in 1999. Ms. Petty, who wore a lapel pin with her daughter's photograph, told Mr. Bush of how the killer even took part in the search for her daughter.

''God bless you,'' Mr. Bush said.

The president also heard from Sharon Brooks of Lancaster, Calif., whose 16-year-old daughter, Tamara, was kidnapped in August with another teenager, Jacqueline Marris, in a nationally publicized abduction. The two were later found through the Amber Alert program, and their abductor, a man identified as Roy Dean Ratliff, was shot to death after resisting when sheriff's deputies pulled over his car and ordered him out.

''The Amber Alert system is, I'm sure, what saved Tamara and Jackie,'' Ms. Brooks said.

Mr. Bush met with Ms. Brooks and the other parents a few blocks from the White House at the Ronald Reagan Building, where the conference was held. Mr. Bush announced the conference this summer as concerns about a rash of kidnappings heightened across the country, even though statistics show that the number of child abductions by strangers has fallen in recent years.

According to the National Center for Missing and Exploited Children, about 100 children are abducted by strangers each year, down from a range of 200 to 300 during the 1980s.

Amber Alert programs have been adopted in at least 20 states in recent months, including New York, New Jersey, California and Florida, and in dozens of smaller areas. The system was named for Amber Hagerman, a 9-year-old girl who was kidnapped six years ago from Arlington, Tex., and killed.

Last month, the Senate passed a bill to provide $25 million to help establish a national Amber Alert system. Mr. Bush urged the House of Representatives to pass a similar measure.

CHAPTER 26
OPRAH
NOVEMBER 2003

Not long after, I received another surprising phone call. This one was from Harpo Studios in Chicago, Illinois. *The Oprah Winfrey Show* was doing an episode on children left home alone: *How young is too young?* I accepted the invitation, but with a bit of hesitation. I felt uncomfortable with the subject matter of the show. I hadn't been the one who left Andi home alone. Besides, what happened to Andi could have just as easily happened if she had been getting off the school bus at the end of the drive or walking through the wooded area to her grandparents' home. I didn't want to bash Greg on national television or be painted as a neglectful parent when my child hadn't even been in my care at the time. I expressed those concerns to the *Oprah* producers, and they assured me that it wouldn't be like that. Oprah just wanted me to come and tell the story to help open dialogue on the subject.

Before I knew it, Melanie and I were on a plane headed for Chicago. When we arrived, a limousine driver was waiting by the baggage claim, holding a cardboard sign with our names on it. After we got into his vehicle, he glanced into his rearview mirror and said, "*Oprah* Show, right?"

"Yes, why?"

He chuckled. "We also do pickups for *The Jerry Springer Show*, and I can always tell the difference between the *Springer* guests and the *Oprah* guests. You are definitely an *Oprah* guest."

"The *Springer* guests act like that in real life?" I asked. "I thought it was all an act."

"Oh no." He shook his head wryly. "What you see on TV is what you get with them. I've had to pull the limo over a few times and threaten to kick them out. *Oprah* guests are always classier. Never have problems with them."

I had never been out of O'Hare Airport in Chicago, so my first glimpse of the city wasn't impressive. The highway led through a huge housing district with the most dilapidated tenement buildings I had ever seen. But then, we entered downtown, and it was like a different world. It was beautiful—the streets were clean, and everyone was bustling from place to place. The limousine driver dropped us off at the All-Suites Omni Hotel, where Oprah always housed her guests. I found during my stay that Oprah's reputation for generosity wasn't exaggerated. We were housed in a suite and afforded a nice meal allowance as well.

The next day, they whisked us away in a different limousine to Harpo Studios. Melanie and I were escorted into "The Green Room," where the walls were lined with photos of Oprah and every celebrity you could imagine—Garth Brooks, Julia Roberts—you name a celebrity, and they were more than likely on that wall. I assumed Oprah would come in and meet us beforehand, but I found this wasn't her custom. Instead, we met with the producer, who told us what to expect. Then, we were directed into a room where make-up artists and hair stylists prepared us for the show. Next, they took us out and sat us in the front row. I remembered thinking that the set was far smaller than it looked on television. There were cameras everywhere, and Oprah's yellow couch was right in front of us—the same couch Tom Cruise would later make his proclamation claiming his love for Katie Holmes. It was all surreal.

After a nerve-wracking 20 minutes in which all the audience guests were seated and final preparations made, Oprah Winfrey herself entered the room to a roar of applause. She immediately made everyone laugh by commenting on her new shoes and how uncomfortable they were. I noticed the red bottom, Christian Louboutin. She soon got to business and began visiting with the invited guests on the front row.

The camera cut back and forth, and everything moved so fast. My heart was beating in my throat. I had done many television and radio interviews with powerful personalities, but for some reason, Oprah's very presence intimidated me. From the moment I saw her, tears threatened to flow from my eyes. Andi had loved *The Oprah Winfrey Show*, and I knew that, in a way, she was meeting her today.

Oprah spoke to several people by the first commercial break, and some of their stories were quite horrifying. One mother had left her small children overnight in an apartment while she went to work, and one of the children had died from a tragic accident while she was gone. Another parent described how they had trusted their teenage daughter alone at home, only to find she was having sex with her boyfriend while they were away. As I listened to these stories, I became even more uncomfortable. How did my story fit into this puzzle? My situation seemed so different. Andi's father had been at a nearby pond, and her grandparents were close by, within shouting distance. What could Oprah's discussion possibly have to gain from my story?

The cameras paused for what would be a commercial break, and during the short break, Oprah pointed at me and motioned for me to come up. No other guest had been invited to sit on the couch with her; I felt paralyzed. She kept motioning, however, and when I sat down on the couch, she took my hand and said, "I really like your shirt!" It was just like regular girl talk.

"Thank you?" I responded. My hand was shaking.

The cameras queued back up, and I could see on the monitors that the big O came up behind Oprah and me. Then, Andi's face came through the O. The tears now spilled down my cheeks. The combination of seeing my daughter's face and knowing she was receiving national exposure and me sitting on the yellow couch with arguably the most powerful woman in the world was almost more than my system could bear. Oprah began asking me questions, and I could do little more than stammer answers. I felt I was not a very good guest during this interview. I was petrified. But thank God for good editing. The producers managed to make me look halfway eloquent, even though I was anything but. It was the most intimidating interview I had ever done.

The rest of the show went by in a blur, and then, when we were being escorted from the studio, Oprah began to bring the guests on the stage to take individual photos with each one. Security buzzed around her, and if I thought the Secret Service had given me the evil eye, I hadn't known the real definition of the term until now. Oprah called me up, and when she found out that Melanie was with me, she motioned for her to come down out of the seats. Melanie stood up in the excitement and hurried to the end of the aisle to come down the steps toward me. As soon as her foot hit the step, one of Oprah's bodyguards rushed to the foot of the aisle and shouted, "SIT DOWN!" When I saw the wounded and stunned expression on my fourteen-year-old daughter's face as she wheeled around like a scared kitten and hurried back to her seat, fury rose in me. Oprah was already distracted by someone else, even though she still had her hand on my shoulder. She had already forgotten about me and my daughter in the bustle around her and hadn't even noticed this exchange. Rather than try to explain, I gave up my chance to have a picture with Oprah Winfrey and headed toward my daughter, whose lip was quivering and eyes were brimming with unshed tears.

"Come on, Mel. It's gonna be alright."

"I hate *The Oprah Winfrey Show*." I chuckled because only an hour before, she had said, "I love *The Oprah Winfrey Show*."

I hugged her, and we joined the line to file out of the studio.

It was an experience that was like none other. The show aired about a month later. There was still so much work to be done. I prepared myself for anything. Being on *The Oprah Winfrey Show*, sitting on the couch next to her, doing something not many people had done, was exciting. However, my desire was to help children and families.

That was the next step, and oh, boy, I was in for some doozies. Helping families who had lost children to predatory crime was an ugly business.

But someone had to do it. But first, we had to face an execution. I had gotten word that it would be happening soon. I was scared.

February 4, 2004

Rebecca DeMauro
3122 N. Country Rd
Skiatook, OK 74070

Dear Rebecca,

Thank you for being a guest on the show.

We appreciate your taking time to share yourself with our
viewers and studio audience.

Sincerely,

Oprah Winfrey

OW/jjb

CHAPTER 27

December 2003

Dear Rebecca Petty,

I once thought, what could I possibly say that would bring you healing for the loss, heartache, and devastation that I caused you. I was compelled by something deep inside for so long to see if you would talk with me if you were given the chance. So that maybe somehow you could hear and see that I'm very sorry and deeply overwhelmed. But, you were not willing. You'll never know what it took for me to even come to that point, to face and talk to you. I am so ashamed and guilt is more than I can bear. Now that I think about it, I realize that seeing me would have been too difficult for you. I don't know how to write emotions, nevertheless I'll try.

I do not ask you to forgive me or to even try. I realize that only Jesus can forgive me or anyone else as far as that goes and only He can bring the comfort and healing that everyone needs. My actions have caused so many people heartache and loss including myself. I am truly sorry for everything. I have no excuse. Therefore, I accept the death penalty as my punishment. I realize how weak and unbecoming any words of mine are to you. Alone, I pray for the day to come, though my Shepherd knows when, I pray death brings a sense of justice done. There is hope for a brighter tomorrow for you and for all.

Karl Roberts

VARNER SUPERMAX
JANUARY 2004

Most people thought they could never kill a person. At one time, I thought the same thing. But at that moment, I knew I could. I could kill another human being—one particular human being—without batting an eye or losing a millisecond of sleep.

But I didn't have to. The state was about to do it for me.

As the hour approached, it seemed the execution was on, and so we were told to go to the Department of Corrections Headquarters. "We" included the Brewer family and my family—my sister, parents, Colleen Nick, Kris, and myself. We arrived, and they ushered us into a large room where they had catered sandwiches, cookies, fruit, and pop. It reminded me of a church social—except who could eat at a time like that? It was like all the food brought when Andi was missing. It was one of those Southern hospitality things. After a brief wait at the DOC Headquarters, they loaded us into a van. We traveled in a convoy with several other vans to the Varner Unit south of Pine Bluff, Arkansas, to Grady, Arkansas, where the only jobs available were working for the prison, flying a crop duster plane, or being a police officer in the speed trap town where if you blinked, you'd miss it. We held on tightly as they drove what I swore approached 100 miles an hour at times down the highway.

"Why are we driving so fast?" I asked.

"When it's not so goddamned cold, we usually have death penalty protesters following us, trying to harass the victim's family," he answered, without moving his eyes from the road, knuckles clenched at ten and two. "That's why we take three or more vans, so no one knows which one the victim's family is actually in."

How comforting. I contained my annoyance by stifling an eye roll, pulling my seatbelt tighter, and holding on.

About 30 miles south of Pine Bluff, the guard put on his blinker and headed toward a huge complex in the middle of a large flat plain. The prison was lit up like a Christmas tree. The vast complex looked menacing.

We pulled up to the prison entrance, and they waved us through; we were driven into a tangled mess of barbed wire as the place was surrounded by security fencing. In the compound, we saw a spattering of the protesters the driver had mentioned, huddled up against the cold, holding up protest signs. I guessed six degrees was *"too goddamn cold,"* keeping all but the most faithful away. Satellite trucks with large dishes pointing upwards from news stations littered the parking lot.

Upon arrival, we met up with Prosecutor Williamson and many familiar faces from the search with the Arkansas State Police, the FBI, and the news media. We were escorted through the security gate, which hummed loudly. Electrified. No one was escaping out of that hellhole. Only five members of our family were allowed in to witness the execution: me, Kris, my sister Kristy, Greg, and Carla.

Later, we found out that our extended family had been escorted to a large tent outside the prison gates with the protesters, where they received a "royal" treatment of dinky space heaters and pocket hand warmers. I found out later that the Arkansas State Police were going to make my extended family sit in their cars. However, Colleen came to the rescue and pled with them to allow them to come into the tent they had set up away from protesters. No dignity had been intended to be shown to any of my family.

We didn't fare much better. We were indoors at least, but instead of being led into the execution chamber, we were escorted into the warden's office: a tiny, dank room filled with a huge oak desk and shelves of books. We were informed that this would be our viewpoint for the execution via closed-circuit television. The prosecutor, police, and news media were taken into the execution chamber.

"What the hell? Are you serious?"

"Sorry, state law," a guard shrugged. I bet he wouldn't have been shrugging had it been his daughter.

Rage was probably the strongest word for anger in the English language, and it could not begin to describe how I felt. How was it that the parents of the murdered child were placed in the warden's office while the prosecutor, the sheriff, the FBI, and God knows who else were seated behind the glass in the execution chamber mere feet from Roberts? I wanted to see that man take his last breath, just as he had seen my daughter take hers. They didn't seem to care that I had given birth to this little girl. I had spent twelve precious years raising her to the best of my ability, and they said a motherfucking state law was going to keep me from attending to the last bit of business my daughter had on this planet? I was livid.

Here you go, one dose of juicy re-victimization, courtesy of the state of Arkansas.

On the six-inch closed-circuit television screen before me was the execution chamber, the Death House, as they called it at the Arkansas State Penitentiary. Our chairs were in a semi-circle in front of the screen, and we all leaned forward to see it. The black and white television set illuminated the stark white walls. A gurney took center stage. On that gurney were two arm boards that stretched out to each side, with Velcro straps hanging in long strips to the side; it looked like a crucifix they had laid down on an ambulance cot. Four more brown belt straps were draped across the gurney: one for the chest area, one for the midsection, and one for each leg. I took all this in. Vivid images snapped through my head. Would he say he was sorry at the end? Would he twitch when he died? Gurgle? Seize? I once saw a mouse get snapped in a trap, and it twitched for a full minute before it was finally still. I remembered being mortified. I had never put a mousetrap out in our house since. How could I have such pity and mercy on a rodent and none for a living human?

My heart began to race, and sweat beads popped out on my forehead and upper lip. I suddenly began to feel an urgency to release this man from the trap and from my hatred. The feeling was so strong that I wanted to scream at the top of my lungs for them to stop this charade. I wrung my hands in my lap and prayed. *For Christ's sake, who am I praying to and why?*

All day we had waited as rumors swirled in Little Rock, anti-death penalty advocates had picketed the governor's mansion, people had seemingly forgotten our little girl who had been left in the woods for three days in the rain naked and raped.

Strangled.

If you take me home, I won't tell my daddy.

This was torture.

There was also talk of Karl's last meal request: four apples, four oranges, four bananas, two pounds of grapes and three bottles of water —an odd request in comparison to the other man who was also scheduled to be executed that same fateful night: two double cheese, double soybean patty sandwiches, fried eggplant, fried green tomatoes, fried sweet potato slices, barbequed baked beans, potato salad, glazed donuts, two vanilla milkshakes, two cokes, cashews and shelled pecans.

As always, the thought of God made me think about the F word. *By the F word, I mean forgiveness.* But at that moment, the word "forgiveness" was more of an expletive to me than the other word could have ever been. I had always thought I would never forgive this wrong that had been done to me, never move on until retribution was fully exacted on the one who dealt me the most life-crushing blows. The only thing I'd been interested in would come from the end of that needle filled with sodium thiopental, potassium chloride and pancuronium bromide. Nothing, *I believed,* could equal the thrill that would overtake me when I saw evil take its last, shuddering breath.

Then the phone rang. The guard answered and then looked at us with pity, lowered his eyes, and said, "That was Governor Huckabee. We have a stay of execution."

My heart fell into my stomach, that awful dropping sensation. The F-word faded into the furthest chamber of my being, driven back by the hatred that swelled up like vomit. I could taste it. I could feel it in my eyes. Kris took my hand. I jerked it away. Where was this coming from? Only moments ago, I had felt pity for the man about to be strapped down in the next room. Now, I only wanted him to die.

Everything around me melted, and I was standing at a crossroads, one I did not expect to encounter that day. Where did I go from there? What was I supposed to do? I could try to make the magic again, try to push for execution, putting my health and my marriage at risk and pouring my energies into fulfilling what had been my mission in life for almost five years. I could hide away, letting bitterness slowly suck me under like mud in a river bottom. Or I could face the F-word head-on and try to make peace with it.

Of the three, the third choice sounded the easiest. They may have said, "To err is human, to forgive is divine," but I could tell you that I was very much human and not at all divine. I made the choice. I wanted to see the man who brutalized us die an agonizing death, and to those who expected me to drop my grudge and let bygones be bygones, I had only one thing to say:

F you.

And it didn't stand for forgiveness.

We discovered later why the execution was stayed. Apparently, the ACLU had "gotten to him," and in the calculating manner for which they were famous—and everybody knew it—they had talked him into appealing his sentence after he had spent the last five years waiving his right to appeal.

Arkansas law gives an automatic appeal to those who receive

a sentence of death. He didn't want it for five years. Had petitioned the court to waive it, been granted that waiver. Now on the eve of facing his Maker as a child rapist and killer, he couldn't do it. Could not accept his punishment. I was thinking about his letter to me.

Therefore, I accept the death penalty as my punishment.

Liar.

What a coward. A piece of shit coward.

JANUARY 7, 2004

VARNER, Arkansas (CNN) -- Charles Singleton, a convicted murderer with a history of severe mental illness who had been on Arkansas' death row longer than any other inmate, was put to death Tuesday by lethal injection for killing a woman during a robbery.

Witnesses described Singleton convulsing slightly and coughing after the drugs were administered.

According to a statement read by Dinah Tyler, spokeswoman for the Arkansas Department of Correction, the injection was administered at 8:02 p.m. Singleton was pronounced dead at 8:06 p.m. at Cummins Prison, about 70 miles south of Little Rock.

Singleton's attorney, Jeffrey Rosenzweig, described himself as "frustrated, disappointed, saddened" by the execution.

Before the execution, when asked if he wanted to make a final statement, Singleton, 44, said, "I was going to speak, but I wrote it down. I'll leave it up to the warden."

Tyler later read Singleton's written statement, which was a largely rambling missive peppered with Biblical references.

"As it is written, I will come forth as you will go," part of the statement said. "I too am going to take someone's place. You've taught me what you want done and I will not let you down. God bless, Charles Singleton," the statement concluded.

Singleton's last meal, eaten Tuesday evening, was mostly vegetarian, prison officials said. He also consumed a milkshake and a few soft drinks. Singleton had met with family members and his spiritual adviser earlier in the day.

Meanwhile, the scheduled execution of another Arkansas inmate Tuesday night was uncertain.

Karl Roberts, convicted of the 1999 kidnapping, rape and murder of his 12-year-old niece, filed a motion just hours before the scheduled 9 p.m. execution by lethal injection. Roberts has not exhausted the appeals in his case but has never before made a move to avoid the death penalty.

His stay was granted Tuesday by the 8th U.S. Circuit Court of Appeals. State Attorney General Mike Beebe filed an appeal of the stay, which was rejected. His office is now considering whether to appeal to the Supreme Court, spokesman Matt DeCample said.

Roberts' warrant for execution expired at midnight.

CHAPTER 28
YOU MESSED WITH THE WRONG KID
MARCH 2006

I had settled down from the "non-execution." I tried not to think about Roberts and just moved forward with raising my girls and doing child advocacy work. Things were changing in the world, and the age of social media was becoming a thing.

Kristin was now ten years old, and Xanga, a social network website, was all the rage with the kids. I had learned in my child advocacy work that there were dangers on the internet, but Kristin wanted to participate with her friends. I sat down with her and helped her set up an account. I used all the safety precautions I had learned. Our computer was set up in a central location, the dining room, so that I could see everything she was looking at. I had discussed the pitfalls and dangers of the internet with both of my girls and coached them on what to do if anyone made inappropriate contact with them.

Since that time, many safeguards had been set up to protect children from online predators, but in 2006, social networking was a fairly new trend, and the kinks were still being worked out. Kristin's page was very simple, with a couple of pictures of her face and another small picture of her sticking her tongue out at her brother. There was nothing that would cause anyone to target her... or so I thought.

Only a few days after I set up her account, Melanie was helping Kristin play an online computer game when an instant message popped up from "xxitwasntme." The message said, "How are you?" Kristin didn't say anything back because she didn't know who it was, and then she grew a little afraid when another message popped up that said, "You're pretty." Melanie, who was seventeen, called to me and said, "Mom, some guy is bothering us."

I went straight to the computer and sat down. I started typing messages, pretending to be Kristin so that I could find out who it was. Initially, I thought it was a family member playing a prank. After a couple of sentences, I got a creepy feeling and realized this was not anyone we knew, but that he somehow knew about Kristin. Still thinking I was Kristin, he sent me the link to a webcam and said, "Click here."

By this time, I was so angry that I clicked the link. The webcam went straight to his face. He appeared to be in his mid-forties or early fifties with gray hair, a gray mustache, and blue eyes.

"I see you," I typed.

When I said that, he batted the camera away, and it fell to the desk. I could see what I thought were images of a young girl lying on the surface.

I chose this moment to reveal who I was.

"I'm not Kristin," I said. "I'm her mother. I don't know who you are, but I'm getting ready to call the police."

"Please, don't do that," he responded.

Something told me in my gut to send Kristin from the room. I was so glad that I did because, at that moment, the man slowly lifted each picture. In horror, I saw they were pictures of Kristin's Xanga account, and all of them had been enlarged to printer-paper size. When he reached the picture of Kristin sticking her tongue out at Kristofer, he repositioned the camera to focus on his naked crotch. Within seconds, I realized in horror that he was masturbating, looking at Kristin's photo.

By this time, I had already dialed 911, and I was screaming into the phone for the police to get there. Kristin was yelling from the other room, "Take a screenshot! Take a screenshot!"

How did she even know what that meant? She was ten.

"How?" I yelled. I suddenly realized that Kristin was behind me, and I covered the screen with my hands as she pushed the necessary keyboard buttons to snap several screenshots using the print screen button.

This move would prove to be crucial as "xxitwasntme"

signed off before the police arrived at the house. Along with my description of the first sight of the man and Melanie's description of the room behind him, the screenshot helped police locate the man who had targeted Kristin.

I later found out that the police had no idea what to expect when they entered my home. They had been standing behind the dispatcher when my call came in and had only stood long enough to hear my screams and to get the address. For all they knew, they were walking into a murder scene. They didn't realize they were walking into a cyber mess that would take months to unravel.

I hadn't really known what to expect of the man's location, but I thought he could be from anywhere. The officers took our computer to the Tulsa Cyber Crimes Unit so they could pinpoint the location of the predator. Through a multi-county grand jury subpoena for the information on Yahoo ID "xxitwasntme," it was revealed that the identification belonged to Jerry L. Martin of Tulsa, Oklahoma.

Tulsa? That was only 20 miles from our home! It also revealed that another girl from Tulsa had been targeted as well, with much the same story and descriptions. Like Kristin, she had listed her name and birthday on her Xanga account, and like Kristin, had unwittingly chosen a background page that unknowingly revealed these facts to strangers. The thought that this man knew where Kristin lived and that he could have been—and probably was— planning to meet her brought back all the panic from when Andi was kidnapped. At that time, I was helpless. This time, however, I was not.

From the night "xxitwasntme"—also known as "whaazzaaap," "jrrrry," "liiiissaa," "manniiaaccc," and "glitterdunn"—appeared in our life, I was determined that he would be found and stopped from victimizing any other families. I worked closely with the Skiatook Police Department to keep the case moving. With much red tape due to jurisdictional issues, the channels were cleared to search Jerry L. Martin's residence. The following is the Incident Report of the search, prepared by Officer Shane Thompson:

On 5-17-06 at approximately 0700 hours, I, Officer Shane Thompson, along with Lieutenant James Dean, Sergeant Travis Foster, Officer Tracy Moore, Reserve Officers Jerry Bullard, along with Detectives Don Holloway and Richard Coleman from the Tulsa Police Cyber Crimes Unit served a search warrant at _____ in the city of Tulsa, County of Tulsa.

Upon our arrival, we knocked on the door and at this time, a person from inside asked who was there and we notified them that it was the police. We were then met by (female, name withheld) and immediately after by Jerry L. Martin. We then notified them we had a search warrant. I then served Mr. Martin a true and correct copy of the warrant to him personally.

At this time, personal information on the suspect, as well as his girlfriend, was taken and the search began. The search at the residence began at the southwest bedroom closet to the front of the house. In this room, there was located a Gateway Computer, CPU, with a Gateway 17-inch flat screen monitor. With a Logitech web camera, a Kodak DX 3600 Digital Camera, a Kodak Digital Camera docking station, Gateway Keyboard, a Boston three-piece speaker system, RCA surge suppressor, Logitech mouse, and Efficient Networks Speed Stream Ethernet Modem, as well as a Hewlett Packard Scanner, Printer, Copier, and a bag of shredded papers found in the shredder. The room had yellowish drapes and was small, with white paint on the walls. All evidence was photographed and taken as evidence.

The search then moved into the master bedroom of the residence where there was in the headboard...on the east side...a pair of Harley Davidson handcuffs. Inside of the west side of the bed in the bottom drawer was located numerous Playboy Magazines, along with one unmarked video cassette and a pornographic DVD titled Young, Sweet and Juicy as well as a bandana...as well as a blue full-face ski mask. Inside the master bedroom closet were located six unmarked video cassettes. All evidence items were photographed and taken except for the commercial DVD and the Playboy Magazines.

As the search continued, we then checked the living room where there was located a black and color Samsung camera cell phone, which contained sixteen pictures, one of which was a young girl in a two-piece bathing suit, sitting on a motorcycle. Also located *was a PSO/AEP bill which had Jerry Martin and <address> which shows dominion and control.*

We then searched the bathroom and the kitchen including all cabinets with negative results. We then searched the detached garage of the residence and inside there was located on the east wall of the garage in a cabinet five pairs of soiled underwear in various colors as well as a large amount of cash estimated at 15,000 dollars. Inside the attic area of the detached garage was found an old Stevens model 124C 12-gauge shotgun with no known serial number located. The shotgun did not appear to be in working order. At this time the items were photographed, and the women's underwear were taken as evidence.

I then spoke with Mr. Martin and advised him that he was not under arrest and was not going to be placed under arrest. He stated that he understood. I then asked him about the incident that had occurred in Skiatook on March 8. He stated he did not know what I was talking about. I then advised him of the evidence that was collected previously, "I don't think I did anything illegal." I then asked him if he does this often or is this the only time and he would not answer but did say, I don't do that all the time. I then asked if he was aware that the person that he made contact with on the date was a ten-year-old girl and he stated, "People on the internet are not always who they say they are." I then asked if he talks to young girls often and he would not make a statement. He then stated that he doesn't think he did anything wrong. I then asked if he checked the profiles and if he would still talk to them if they were young and he stated, "On the internet, people are not who they say they are." Mr. Martin was evasive in all his answers and frequently would not answer questions. He consistently repeated the two phrases, "People on the internet are not who they say they are," and "I don't believe I did anything illegal." At this time, I concluded the interview with him.

At approximately 11:30 hours, I was contacted by Detective Holloway and he began the forensic exam of the computer and located a couple of videos from a web camera depicting young girls with an estimated age of 10 to 12 years old showing their breasts to the camera. He further stated that there were numerous pictures downloaded from sites like Xanga. I then forwarded the copies of the pictures of the victim that were posted on her website so that he would be able to locate the victim in any of the pictures that the suspect had downloaded. He then advised me that he would contact me as soon as the exam was complete.

I then contacted the victim's mother at approximately 1500 hours. I brought in a photo lineup of a total of six white males, one of which was the suspect and all matching the suspect's description. I then asked her if the person that she saw on the computer the night of March 8 was in this lineup. She looked at the photos and pointed to #5 and stated, "That is him." I then again asked if she was sure that was the same man and she stated yes, I'm sure that's the guy. I then had her initial by her choice, which was picture number #5.

After she made her selection, I noted that picture #5 was in fact the picture of Jerry Lynn Martin. At this time, I placed the photo lineup into evidence.

Shortly after I identified him, they arrested Jerry Lynn Martin. He pleaded guilty to two felonies: an exposure allegation and a count of soliciting a minor to observe the exposure. He was convicted and sentenced to 10 years in prison and 5 years of probation and was required to register as a sex offender for life.

This wouldn't be his first trip to prison. In 1995, he had been charged with indecent exposure, and in 1997, he had pleaded no contest to a charge of indecent exposure and had served about four months in prison, followed by fourteen months of probation—leaving him free to prey upon children.

But when he messed with my daughter, he messed with the wrong kid.

When we went to court a few months later, and in my victim impact statement, I told him, "Today is your day of reckoning, you messed with the wrong kid."

Bastard.

CHAPTER 29
SHE LOVED EVERYONE SHE MET
PURCELL, OKLAHOMA
APRIL 2006

Seven years after losing Andi, she was never far from my thoughts and probably never would be. However, over the years, the sting had lost some of its sharpness. I was empowered by my child advocacy and the grief work I did for families in a local funeral service, though at times, certain cases I encountered with Team HOPE and the cases where families called me directly for help brought everything rushing back. I did everything I could to help those families, from staying on the phone until the wee hours of the morning just talking and listening to parents' cries, to going to court with them. But my greatest strength seemed to be in helping families deal with the media and forcing the public to look at the victim instead of the perpetrator.

One thing I noticed was that killers and abductors always got top billing from the press. Parents of a child often retreated into themselves, dealing with the media being the last thing anyone wanted to deal with. As a result, the victim got lost in a sea of words, words in which all the attention was focused on the gruesome crime and its perpetrator.

So, in April of 2006, when I watched the news about the abduction and murder of 10-year-old Jamie Rose Bolin in Purcell, Oklahoma, I not only saw the sensationalistic way in which the press handled it but also that her father, Curtis Bolin, had retreated completely into isolation. I felt I had to do something to help him. The heaviness on my heart was so pressing that I could only attribute it to God Almighty himself pushing me to drive across the state to talk to Mr. Bolin. I did not know this man from Adam.

Jamie Rose's story was particularly grisly, involving a cannibalistic plot. Of course, every headline published about Jamie Rose's abduction and murder was insensitive and horrifying. The predator had lured the young girl into his apartment during the short time she was alone after school each day. He had raped and murdered her, keeping her body in an ice-filled tub for days, planning to cannibalize her after barbequing her on his small charcoal grill. I could not fault her father for never going back to his apartment complex. He was more than likely suffering from complete shock and hiding out from the world. It became my mission to find him. Jamie's aunt had somehow heard about me and my advocacy work, and she contacted me, asking me to come and help the family cope. I agreed to go to Purcell.

Purcell, the county seat of McClain County, Oklahoma, had a population of 6,500 and was a relatively safe community south of Oklahoma City. Before Jamie Rose was murdered, I had barely heard of, much less visited, this small Oklahoma town. When I arrived, I had no clue where to find Curtis, so I stopped at a hole-in-the-wall convenience store and asked if there was a hotel in town—Curtis had reportedly refused to go back to his apartment above the crime scene where Jamie Rose's body had been found. The clerk told me there was only one and gave me directions.

I drove up to the small, one-story hotel, expecting to have to search for Mr. Bolin as I had been warned about his reclusive behavior. When I pulled all the way into the parking lot, I noticed one hotel door open.

"God, it can't be this easy, can it?" I whispered to myself. I turned the car off and stared for a moment at the open door, hoping someone would step out. When no one did, I took a deep breath, realized I might be losing my mind, and opened the car door. I walked up and stuck my head inside. There was a man standing there.

"Curtis Bolin?" I asked.

The man's eyes grew suspicious, and he cocked his head sideways. "I'm Curtis. But if you're a reporter, you need to leave."

Suddenly, I was a bit frightened. I knew what it was like to be approached at a moment like this when all you wanted was to be left alone. But I opened my mouth and introduced myself, telling him who I was and why I was there. His demeanor softened, and the stiffness faded with my words. He visibly relaxed as he realized that, for the moment, I was a kindred spirit. Within a few moments after that, he not only hugged me but also began to cry. I stood there and just held him, letting his tears flow. I knew it was time for me to be strong for him, so I stifled back my own tears. When he stood upright and wiped his face, he could barely speak. I motioned for him to sit on the edge of the bed, and I pulled up a chair in front of him. Again, the thought crossed my mind that I was alone with a strange man in a hotel room in the middle of a town I had never been to.

Then he started talking about Jamie Rose: what a good girl she was, what she liked, how everyone loved her. Tears wet his eyes again.

Next, he relayed how frustrated he was with the media and how they wouldn't leave him alone. This was not news to me. I had heard this over and over from families I had been assigned to help with Team HOPE.

I took him by the hand. "Curtis, look at me."

He brought his blue eyes up to meet mine. They were puffy from lack of sleep and crying, and I could almost see his shattered soul through the window of his eyes. At the same time, both eyes dropped a single tear simultaneously.

"I'm going to say something to you that is going to be very hard to hear. Your little girl sounds so wonderful. She's beautiful with red hair and freckles. She's sweet and kind and lovely. But right now, no one is hearing all that. All they are hearing is how this man, this monster, wanted to eat her." I hated with every inch of my being that I had to be so blunt. However, I knew I was the only person on the planet who could speak frankly to this man at this moment in time.

Curtis began to nod his head. Surprisingly, he agreed with me.

I went on. "They need to hear the good things about her. And only you can tell them that. If you don't say anything, it's all going to be about her murderer. We want everyone to know about her."

"How do I do that? I want everyone to know her," he said. "I want them to know that I believe she's in heaven playing checkers with my dad..." He continued, words pouring out of him about her politeness, her inquisitiveness, her sweet nature. Soon, he was sobbing again. He wiped his face.

"I want them to know she loved everyone she met."

Within the hour, he decided to talk to *The Daily Oklahoman.* I sat next to him and held his hand while he took control, taking charge of his power, if only for a few moments. I was so proud of him.

The next day, instead of the headline talking about the

cannibalistic murderer, the headline read:

'She loved everybody she met.' Slain Girl's Father Struggles with Grief in Purcell

When I read the story, I cried again; I knew God had led me right to Curtis Bolin.

Later, I met with the rest of the family to gather pictures and videos of Jamie Rose to make her *Celebration of Life* video montage. It was a beautiful tribute. I gauged that there were over 1,000 people at her funeral in the high school gymnasium. Helping her dad and making a video to honor her life was the least I could have done for this precious girl's family.

Two years later, on February 29, 2008, a jury found Kevin Ray Underwood guilty of first-degree murder. A jury recommended the death penalty on March 7, 2008. On April 3, 2008, McClain County District Judge Candace Blalock approved the recommended death sentence.

NOVEMBER 2007
TULSA, OKLAHOMA

While the Jamie Rose Bolin case had been one of the more intense encounters in my work as an advocate, the search for Cori Baker was the most emotionally charged and physically draining event I had ever encountered regarding a missing child—apart from my own daughter, Andi's, case.

In November of 2007, thirteen-year-old Cori went missing in Tulsa. School surveillance cameras had captured her getting into her older sister's boyfriend's car that Friday afternoon. When she didn't arrive home as expected, her father, Daniel, called the police. Police automatically assumed she was a runaway and put him off until Monday, which was when word of the incident reached me.

A local television reporter contacted me and asked me to come and help the father of 13-year-old Cori, as he was having a very difficult time. I went and visited with Daniel Baker, just as I had with Jamie Rose Bolin's father, and found that he had the same issues with the media as Curtis Bolin. He didn't want to talk to them, didn't appreciate their intrusion, and wanted to be left alone. He had even slammed the door in their faces, yelling, "Go away!"

I talked to him for a little bit, trying to calm him down and explain that he needed the media.

"I don't need them; they just want to intrude."

"Well, Daniel, what do you want most right this second if you could have anything in the world?" I asked.

"I want my daughter to come home." Tears fell down his cheeks.

"How do you propose to do that without the media's help? They are your only avenue to get her picture and all the information out."

It was as if I had slapped him. "I—I don't know."

"The media can be your friend or foe… let's make them our friends. Let's make this about Cori, not about the man who took her."

"How? I don't know how to do this."

I thought about all the other missing child cases I had learned about over the years.

"Let's have a candlelight vigil. Let's make poster boards. Let's put her picture up everywhere." Suggestions began pouring from me, flowing from all the years of experience that had been forced upon me.

"Where can we do it?" he asked. "Won't that take a lot of planning?"

"No. All we need to do is go buy a bunch of candles, get the signs made up, and plan to do this on your front lawn. Then we call the media. They'll show up, trust me."

"You think they'll show up? Really?"

I nodded. "I know they will."

And they did. Every station in town showed up at the candlelight vigil on Cori Baker's front lawn, along with about a hundred other people. With that, the story became about the little girl who was missing instead of her sister's predatory boyfriend. Cori Baker now had a face; she was more than just some missing kid on the news. She became Tulsa's child. Now, we just had to find her.

Her abductor, Marquis Bullock, had been questioned extensively and had convinced police that he and Cori had been walking along the Arkansas River when she had slipped, fallen in, and drowned. Police dragged the river for two days to no avail, then called off the search.

That didn't deter me.

I started calling people I knew. My rants took me to my friends at The Laura Recovery Center out of Friendswood, Texas. They were more than eager to come and help set up a large, organized search. The police department was nothing short of pissed at me, but I didn't care. Everyone had figured out that, by this time, we probably weren't searching for a living child. The evidence seemed to point otherwise. But I understood the importance of knowing what had happened to your child and being able to give that child a decent and proper burial. Alive or not, Cori Baker deserved to be found and brought home.

It turned into a huge endeavor, the largest I had ever been involved in. We called for volunteers to meet at the Oral Roberts University Mabee Center, which became the search headquarters. The Laura Recovery Center arranged it all, putting people to work, taking calls, talking to the media, and organizing searches. They set up grids radiating out from Bullock's apartment across the city and assigned searchers to each grid. We searched. And we searched. And searched some more.

They assigned me a section of the Arkansas River. As an avid kayaker, I didn't balk at this, but it was harder than I had ever imagined it would be. The day was blustery and cold, with typical Oklahoma wind. I rowed and searched every nook and cranny of my given section of the grid. The river was low in some places and high in others. The wind was blowing, and the wake of the water splashed up over the bow of my kayak, drenching me over time. I had never been so wet and cold. The frigid air and water seeped right down into my bones. I wore gloves, but my fingers felt like ice cubes and could hardly curl around my oar. I maneuvered my boat through mud and muck, turning my nose away from the stench that came off the Arkansas. This was one of the murkiest rivers I had ever been on, as it swirled across and cut through the red Oklahoma clay. I searched, feeling anticipation in my gut, and briefly considered how I might feel if I found a dead child floating in this murky mess, but I did not find anything that day. Only trash littered along the bank.

Finally, I covered my entire assigned area and headed back to search headquarters. I pulled my boat up a drainage canal. That's when my foot slipped in the muck, and I fell flat on my back, striking my head on the concrete ditch. Pain shot across my head; I felt nauseous. For a moment, I lay there with my eyes closed in utter defeat—not just from the fall, but from the frustration of not being able to find this little girl after I had done everything physically, mentally, and emotionally possible to do so. I was muddy, mad, and cold.

I looked upward to the sky and yelled at the top of my lungs, "Fuck!"

I immediately felt guilty for saying it. When I opened my eyes, I saw the top of the bank, a walkway lined with people, all of whom had seen me fall. All who had heard my profanity to the sky. No one said a word. They all just stared for a moment, then turned and walked away. I knew they were silent out of respect for me, having seen my orange Laura Recovery Center vest. It wasn't my finest moment.

I just wanted to go home.

Cori Baker's body was found the following March. When the full story was revealed, it was shown that her sister's boyfriend, Marquis Bullock, had lured her into his car with the promise that they were going shopping for a present for her sister's birthday. The rest of the details were sketchy, but it was believed that he had raped and murdered her and then disposed of her body in a paintball park in Sapulpa, Oklahoma. She was found, not by the Laura Recovery Center, not by me in my kayak on the Arkansas River, not by local law enforcement—or even by the famous psychic who had claimed to know her whereabouts—but by a paintball park employee. I cried when I heard the news.

When it was over, I was proud of myself, even though I had angered law enforcement. I had also helped the family of a little girl, even assisting in her funeral by creating a memorial video presentation for her family. Most of all, I had once again helped turn the focus from the killer to the victim, which, to me, was the most important thing—giving the victim a voice.

Jamie Rose and Cori would always be remembered and honored. Most of all, always loved and never forgotten.

CHAPTER 30
2008

Life took a drastic turn after I had kayaked the dirty Arkansas River in search of little Cori Baker's body. I kept up my child advocacy work, never turned down a television interview, continued fighting for children, and worked with families and law enforcement. I also helped people by creating celebration-of-life videos for a funeral service and assisted part-time during visitations and funerals. I understood grief, so I wasn't uncomfortable in the funeral business.

I worked hard to attain my college degree. I wanted to be more than just the grieving mother. I craved a college degree to legitimize the work I was doing. I also changed my major to Criminal Justice. I learned that keeping myself busy and raising my two girls kept me from thinking about appeals in Roberts' case.

Then, heartbreak struck again. On the eve of becoming empty nesters, Kris and I separated. We had stuck it out for nearly ten years after Andi had been murdered, but, in the end, it proved to be too much for us to handle. A once beautiful marriage filled with laughter and happiness had technically died on May 15, 1999, right along with Andi—right along with life as we knew it. Our divorce was final in 2010.

I moved to Rogers, Arkansas, not far from the place my great-grandparents had lived on Beaver Lake. I had spent many summers swimming, boating with family and friends, and sitting on the large front porch of their cabin. The smell of the Arkansas dirt and pine trees was home to me. I had always known in my heart of hearts that I would end up in Arkansas. It had always been the one place on earth where I felt the safest, the most like home.

All through our marriage, I had voiced a desire to retire to the city of Rogers near the lake one day. What I didn't know was that Kris did not have this desire and had never told me he had no intention of *ever* doing so—until we hit Splitsville, USA.

I finished my bachelor's degree in Criminal Justice at Arkansas Tech University *Magna Cum Laude* and consulted for the National Amber Alert program through Fox Valley Technical College, traveling all over the nation.

After I had settled in Arkansas and started life over, I began dating Bill Burnett, a civil engineer who had graduated high school from Hatfield, Arkansas, and was the same age as me. We had a lot in common—both starting over in our late thirties, knowing many of the same people, and liking a lot of the same things. He was good for me. He was kind, gentle, and quiet. I fell pretty hard for him, and we had a lot of fun together. Most importantly, he wasn't afraid of the baggage I carried regarding Andi.

Life began to look up. Then, one day, out of nowhere, I started thinking about how Karl Roberts had avoided his execution day back in 2004 and how poorly the state of Arkansas had treated me and my family. I hadn't spoken of the incident for years, but for some reason, I brought it up with Bill and his friend Daniel while we were talking about politics one day at lunch. I told them about feeling victimized again over that issue and how hurtful it had been when the prison guard shrugged and nonchalantly said, "Sorry, state law," referring to the reason family members could not be present to see the last bit of business a loved one had on this planet.

I would never forget Daniel's face when he said, "You know, Becca, laws can be changed."

He stopped me in my tracks. I stared at him for a moment, speechless. I honestly had never thought for one second about fighting to change that antiquated law. I didn't know why—it had just never crossed my mind.

But Daniel really got the wheels turning in my head.

CHAPTER 31
WALKING THE MILE
2012

How does one eloquently write about a visit to death row? Maybe I was still a little overwhelmed about being invited by the Department of Corrections to be shown around the hellhole called the SuperMax prison in Grady, Arkansas. I called it a hellhole because it was the most depressing, sad, tragic-spirited place ever known to man. This wasn't the first time I had been there, and it certainly wouldn't be the last.

Making the decision to fight to change the law and the way crime victims were treated during the execution of a person who had murdered their loved one turned out to be a difficult process. Plus, capital punishment and executions were a touchy subject for people.

After Daniel reminded me that laws could be changed, he also told me he was friends with Arkansas State Senator Bart Hester and set up a lunch date for us to discuss this issue with him. During our luncheon, Senator Hester didn't touch his meal as I recounted what had happened to us during that cold January day in 2004. He actually *listened* to my plight. I told him how painful the revictimization had been and how important it was for victim families to be able to make their own decisions regarding the process—not be told by a government entity. He seemed to be moved by the story. And upon being sworn into office the following January, true to his word, he wrote Senate Bill 52, the Crime Victims' Rights Bill.

The bill easily made it through the Senate Judiciary Committee and the Senate floor with no opposition. That was when the Department of Corrections took notice. They realized that things would have to change, and they didn't like it one bit. The DOC came out in full force against it. The bureaucrats didn't want their kingdom disturbed. This state agency was not used to playing by the rules; they didn't want the state legislature meddling in their lair. This bill would cause extra work and effort on their part during the execution of a condemned person. They contacted the senator and wanted to meet and talk with the person who was spearheading this "ludicrous bill."

Me.

I was reluctant to meet with them because the bill was going to pass through the House with no problem, right?

However, Senator Hester encouraged me to meet with them so that later, we could say we had exhausted every effort to work with the DOC. But they wanted us to drive to Pine Bluff and meet on their turf. I refused and told Senator Hester that I would only meet with them if they came to Rogers. They didn't like this at all, but I didn't care. I was so over the bullshit of everything: the runaround, the victimization, all of it. I felt grouchy, and I was ready for them to bring it on.

When we sat down with them, I debated about what my family had suffered during the actual crime against my daughter in 1999 and then the "non-execution" in 2004. I showed them Andi's memorial video and several times pointed to her picture, informing them that it was my duty as her mother to see to her final business. They could not argue, really.

Seeing that I wasn't going to budge, they resorted to urging me to beg the senator not to push the bill through. The bill involved building an execution viewing room for the families of crime victims. I didn't care if they hung a sheet to separate the family from the media. To me and all other crime victims, the current law was very unfair. No one should tell a crime victim whether they could or could not view the actual execution. Or dictate how they should or should not deal with their own personal healing. It should be their choice. It should be their right to choose what was best for them— not the state.

Additionally, this wasn't about execution viewing at all; this was about victim choice. And about the Department of Corrections not wanting change. Plus, the fact that they admitted to being attached to some of the death row inmates because they had changed their ways while incarcerated. They had found religion. Praise be to God. They seemed not to support the death penalty at all.

But Karl Roberts had kidnapped, raped, and strangled a child.

They seemed to have forgotten that.

A jury of his peers had convicted him to death by lethal injection, and they seemed to have forgotten about that, too.

Then, something unprecedented happened. They invited us on a private tour to show where the location of the new execution viewing room for crime victims was to be built. Then, they showed us the architectural plans with a price tag of $800,000—which wasn't what we had asked for at all, with only six extra chairs in the current room for the victim's family. How had they already had all this work done? They were ahead of the game and wanted to make the state legislature believe it was all about money when, in reality, it was only about them retaining power and control.

They didn't want some crime victim's mother to come and shake up the way it had always been done.

Everything happened so quickly after that. When Senator Hester and I arrived at the Arkansas Department of Corrections Varner SuperMax, we were met by the warden, several high-end prison officials, and guards. It was much different during this visit, as opposed to the one in 2004, in the shadow of a senator.

They led us through door after door and told us to walk to the left as we were led in front of the solitary confinement area for troubled inmates. "These men would just as soon kill you as look at you," they told me, "so you don't want to even give them a chance to grab you."

My heart raced as I passed; I felt a bit like Clarice Starling in Thomas Harris' *The Silence of the Lambs.*

"I ate his liver with some fava beans and a nice chianti," she had said, walking to the end of the corridor to meet Hannibal Lecter.

They also told me it was possible to be "dashed," meaning having urine, feces, or semen thrown on me. These men behaved like animals. It was frightening. It really was a hellhole.

Then, they took us to the seventy-two-hour holding cell where they housed an inmate about to be executed. There were two very small bluish-colored cells (empty because there were no scheduled executions) with a slab for a bed, a one-inch mattress, a sink, and a toilet. I touched the bars.

The guard said he had the keys—I could go inside if I wanted.

I told him no thanks. I was good.

I had learned about deterrence in my criminal justice classes; for me, this entire experience made me never even want to jaywalk.

I looked at the warden. His expression was blank. I knew he was angry about the change I wanted to implement. That one lone crime victim fighting back, a mom spearheading a campaign, finding a senator who believed in the cause, and doing something to change things just didn't sit well with him.

I knew from the moment I laid eyes on him he was angry, and at first, I was intimidated. But then I thought about Andi—her smile, her giggle. I thought about how long I had been fighting for her, for children who had been kidnapped, raped, and murdered violently. For their rights. For victims' rights.

I stood up straight, put my shoulders back, and decided that he could just get glad in the same pants he got mad in.

He'd live.

She didn't.

Next, we walked the "mile." And I couldn't get the words from Stephen King's *The Green Mile* out of my mind, "Walkin' the mile, walkin' the mile, gettin' right with Jesus, walkin' the mile." Even though I was not a condemned person, that walk was haunting. The walls seemed like a giant throat that swallowed us up.

Then they opened a door, and we were in the execution chamber. The gurney was there in the center of the room. It wasn't any different than the old gurneys I had used back when I was a paramedic. The only difference is this gurney had tie-downs. Leather straps that belted the legs and the arms straight out to the side, fashioned like a crucifix. I wasn't frightened, although I expect they all wanted me to be. I was calm. I knew this would be the place where inmate SK956 would die, where he would take his final breath, here in a controlled environment. Not on the rocky dirt of the forest with sticks and brambles digging into his back. Not in a violent manner where he was cursed, or raped, or choked to death.

Sterile. Clean. Easy.

That's what was waiting for him.

I looked back at the gurney; I reached my hand out to touch it. I wanted to feel how soft the sheets were, then thought better of it. I pulled my hand back. I didn't want them to think I was some kind of sicko. I just wanted to touch it, to see if the sheets are soft, but I refrained.

Then I was led into the execution viewing room where there were 30 chairs lined up neatly for the media, the FBI, law enforcement who worked the case, and the prosecutor, his attorneys, and his spiritual adviser; it had become all about him. And until the changing of this law, there would be no chair for me, her mother who gave birth to her and loves her. No, until I pressed all the way through for change, my place would be in another room to watch via live satellite feed. This was so wrong. I took a seat facing the gurney behind the glass, and they all followed suit. The silence was deafening. We all stared at that gurney. I tried to feel something, anything—but I only had flashes of scenes from Andi's life. Her birth, her jokes, her loving nature, her tormenting her sisters, her eating pickles and home-grown tomatoes, her cute Southern drawl, and I felt ill about what SK956 had done to her.

I could not feel bad for him, no matter how hard I tried. He had made his choice; it wasn't my place to feel bad for him. I had felt bad long enough. I felt bad when the sheriff told me she had been murdered. I felt bad when I had to watch that pink casket lowered into the ground. I felt bad when I had to go to a capital murder trial for my 12-year-old daughter, and I had felt bad for longer than she had been alive.

The warden finally locked eyes with me; they were brown, flecked with gold, and hard behind the rims of his bifocals. I locked my eyes back with his, and I didn't flinch or look away.

"Well?"

"Well, what?"

"You don't want to witness an execution," he said.

"You don't know me. You didn't know my daughter."

"What do you want," he pushed his glasses up his greasy nose.

"I want to see justice served. I want the law changed."

He threw his hands up and broke eye contact. Then the warden asked the senator if that was all we wanted and gazed at his wrist, insinuating it was lunchtime.

Senator Hester turned his face to mine and asked if there was anything else I would like to see on our tour of this facility as a taxpayer of the state of Arkansas. I didn't know why I said what I said next, but it just popped out of my mouth.

"I want to see death row."

The air sucked out of the room, and everyone froze.

"She wants to see death row," Hester said.

They began to scramble and talk on their radios but quickly complied. Technically, the senator was *their* boss. The next thing I knew, I was being escorted by six burly DOC guards towards the death row unit in the Varner Supermax. Walking through the bowels of that prison I was scared but didn't want them to know, so I kept my back straight and my nose up. But, my insides were shaking. Their boots thudded loudly as they led me to SK956's home.

Will I see him? Will he see me?

We made our way across floors so shiny and clean you could eat off them, and when we passed by inmates waxing the floors, they stood and turned their backs to us. We entered through heavy blue steel bars, and the ominous sound of them clanking behind us sent chills down my spine. Once inside, we climbed the long flight of stairs to an indoor bridge with armed guards, the warden, and all the bigwigs. The bridge was two stories high and cut straight down the middle of the SuperMax. We were smack dab in the middle of the most notorious murderers in the state of Arkansas and they were all tucked away in their cubby holes like rats in a cage.

"Help me," someone screamed at the top of their lungs. "I've been framed."

The voice echoed through the hall and reverberated from the ceiling. The loud chatter of the other inmates echoed loudly. It was deafening.

"He screams all day and night," the warden said. "We can't get him to stop. He keeps the others riled up."

I opened my mouth to ask why he was there, but I presumed it was murder and snapped my lips shut.

"So, this is death row," the warden said.

You don't say.

"Where is he?"

The warden cocked his head to the side, squinted his eyes and leaned forward.

"Who, Ms. Petty?"

Was he seriously in charge of this place?

"Karl Roberts?"

Senator Hester straightened and realized what I wanted to see. He knew I needed to see him locked in his cell. I wanted to see justice being served right then. He spoke up.

"Which cell is Karl Roberts housed in?" Hester asked.

Nervous chatter once again ensued as the warden asked the guard manning the control board which cell SK956 was being housed in. She quickly typed in the number and pointed down.

"He's on the bottom, third cell from the left."

I turned and looked and there he was. The monster of my nightmares was leaning forward, looking out the window of his cell door, squinting up at the walkway where I stood. Because of the one-way glass, he couldn't see me, but he noticed the commotion and squinted nonetheless as he tried to figure out what was going on. He never knew I was up there, and after a few minutes, he turned away and began to pace back and forth in that very small room.

Back and forth.

He looked like a caged rat pacing, and for a moment, I almost felt sorry for him. He looked like an animal in a cage, and the thought of having nothing to do every day except pace like a caged animal was beyond comprehension for me. I was so confused by my emotions. Then it hit me again and I realized why he was there. He was a child rapist and murderer. The words in his confession sent shockwaves through my head.

"I mashed my thumbs in her throat, and I squeezed until her face turned blue, and she went limp, quit moving, quit fighting."

When those words entered my mind, all sympathy for him left. He could have stopped this at any time in the commission of his crime but didn't.

I watched him pace for a few more minutes and then told Senator Hester I had seen enough.

A few weeks later, the Arkansas House of Representatives made their decision. Senate Bill 52, the Crime Victims' Rights Bill, failed by one vote after the Department of Corrections convinced the house members that the bill was all about money and a vengeful mother.

I cried like a baby when the bill failed.

And I told myself I was done fighting.

CHAPTER 32
2014
STILL STANDING

Two years passed, and I knew the legislature was going back into session in 2015. I picked up the phone and called Senator Hester, asking if he would consider running the bill again—this time, without the price tag of building a separate room for the victims' families. I told him I would donate a bed sheet or a shower curtain to separate the families from the media and law enforcement. He laughed. I was kidding.

Kind of.

Then, he asked me a question that changed the course of my life—as though it hadn't been changed enough.

"What's your address?"

"What do you mean?"

"Where do you live? Your physical address."

I told him, and he said to hang on a minute. When his voice came back on the line, he told me my address fell in the Ninety-Fourth District and that my state representative was leaving office due to term limits.

"Okay?"

"Well, why don't you run for office and pass the bill yourself? You be the House sponsor, and I'll sponsor it in the Senate. We can call it *Andi's Law.* We can right all these wrongs."

"I'm not a politician, Senator."

"Neither was I. But I ran for the Senate, and here I am. You can do this."

When I gave it some more thought, I realized I was in a place where I actually *could* do it. My girls were grown and out on their own. I was doing consultant work, had a college degree, and could pick and choose when and where I worked. Except for the fact that I had no idea how to be a politician, what was stopping me?

I decided to do it.

Bill and I had since moved in together, and when I told him I was going to go for it, he looked at me as if I had lost my ever-loving mind.

"Well, Cookie," he said, using his pet name for me, "shouldn't you start with the school board or city council?"

"Why?"

"I don't know. Because that's how most people do it."

"You should know by now that I'm not *most* people. I know we aren't married, but I would love to have your support in this."

He nodded slowly, rubbing his chin in deep thought. Then, he looked at me with eyes as green as emeralds.

"Okay, I'm all in."

On March 3, 2014, we drove to Little Rock, and I filled out the paperwork to run for State Representative of the Ninety-Fourth District of Arkansas. I made the rounds of the different tables, signing my life away to take this momentous journey.

Let me assure you—filling out the paperwork was the easiest part of running for office.

But I cherished every moment of it.

After I finished, I walked out onto the lawn of the Arkansas State Capitol, slipped off my shoes, and dug my feet into the dirt—just like I had done at the White House in Washington, D.C. Moments like this didn't come around every day, and I *knew* I was making history. I wanted my feet in the dirt.

This time, my sister Kristy joined me on the lawn, and Bill snapped our picture.

That image still makes me smile.

The real work began after that. With only two months before the primary election, we had our work cut out for us. District 94 was home to 30,000 people, and while I couldn't knock on 30,000 doors, Bill drove me all over the district, and we sure tried.

We sent mailers, ate breakfast with veterans at the American

Legion, and planted *Rebecca Petty* campaign signs on just about every corner. When the grass around them got high, Bill dragged out his weed-eater and slick the grass around them. When he said he was *all in,* I quickly learned that *all in* for him meant *win.* I loved him even more for that.

I won the Primary Election. And a couple of months later, Bill asked me to marry him.

I said *yes,* and we married on the Caribbean island of St. Lucia in the West Indies.

CHAPTER 33

We had won the Primary Election, but we were quickly headed for the General Election, and I was up against a retired teacher who had taught nearly every person in District 94 for the last 35 years. What did that mean? More door knocking, more mailers, and even more campaigning. By the time November 2014 rolled around, I was dead tired.

On election night, Senator Hester invited Bill and me into his home to watch the results roll in with his wonderful family. I had never been so nervous. The numbers began pouring in, and reality sank in—I was winning, and I was winning *big*.But I still couldn't believe it. It felt surreal.

I chewed my nails to the quick while everyone else laughed, snacked, and celebrated. I sat on the couch, fidgeting, when suddenly my favorite band, Foo Fighters, came on during a show we were watching. The election ticker scrolled across the screen, results flooding in. I pulled out my phone and snapped a picture.

It was in that moment I realized—my opponent had no way to recover from the beating I had given him. All the hard work had paid off. I was too far ahead for him to catch me.

I cried and my campaign manager, Keith, called me and said, "Congratulations, Representative."

I was State Representative-elect, and in January, I was going to Little Rock.

My first order of business as the newly elected representative of the 94th District of Arkansas…**ANDI'S LAW.**

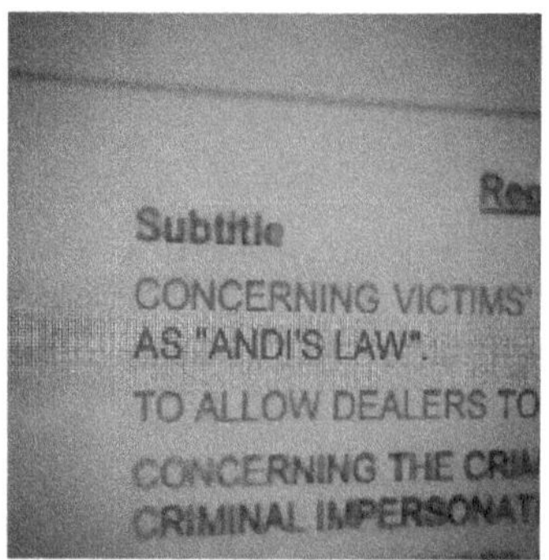

Rebecca Petty, Arkansas lawmaker whose daughter was murdered, sees executions as end of long wait.

(Washington DC) The Arkansas plan to execute multiple murderers over 11 days before a lethal injection drug expires has been condemned as a reckless rush to judgment, but that's not how Rebecca Petty sees it.

The Republican state legislator has been waiting 17 years for Arkansas to put to death the man who murdered her 12-year-old daughter. Even though he has been on death row since 2000, he isn't one of the seven men scheduled to die by lethal injection from April 17-27.

"There are all these victims' families out there who have been — I don't want to say 'waiting,' but who have had this hanging over their heads for the last two decades," said Ms. Petty. "That's how I look at it."

Her daughter Andria Nichole Brewer was raped and strangled by an uncle by marriage in May 1999, her body found after a three-day search in the woods near her father's home in rural Arkansas.

"I don't see it as rushed when a jury sentenced them

to death two decades ago," Ms. Petty said. "To say it's rushed — from a victim's point of view, it seems like 'it's time.'"

Still, hers is something of a voice in the wilderness. The compressed time frame has generated national outrage from death penalty foes urging Arkansas Gov. Asa Hutchinson to stop the "assembly line" schedule, saying it violates the prisoners' rights and increases the possibility of mistakes.

Ms. Petty, 47, knows from experience how quickly the tide can turn on death row.

On Jan. 6, 2004, she sat in an Arkansas prison awaiting the execution of Karl D. Roberts, her daughter's killer. Although he had insisted for years that he would not appeal his sentence, he changed his mind at the last minute and was granted a stay.

"Gov. [Mike] Huckabee ended up signing the death warrant, and they said we could come to the prison, and they set the execution date, and at the very, very last minute, he decided that he wanted his appeal," Ms. Petty

recalled.

The experience would lead her to her life's work: fighting for crime victims and their families. On that day at the prison, she was stunned at how she was treated: She wasn't allowed to witness the execution in person, and only five of her relatives were permitted in the building.

"When we got there, they took us off to the warden's office, where they put us on a closed-circuit feed to watch it. I was just like, 'You've got to be kidding,'" Ms. Petty said. "The TV set they had was like from the 1950s, all green and grainy. I was just so stunned. When I came out of there, I was just fuming."

On top of that, she said, "my family wasn't treated well. They weren't even allowed on the prison grounds. It was like 2 degrees outside, and my family was outside in this little tent, freezing, and we were inside in this cramped warden's office, and I thought, 'This is just crappy.' It was so traumatizing that I didn't speak about it for 10 years."

When she finally told a friend about that day, he urged her to contact her state senator and push for reform.

A bill on behalf of victims' families made it through committee but died on the House floor.

The state senator encouraged her afterward to run for office, and she did, winning a seat in the Arkansas House in 2014. Her bill, called Andi's Law, passed in 2015 without a dissenting vote despite the opposition of officials with the state Department of Corrections.

"They just didn't want it to be a big spectacle. They came up with, 'We need to spend $5 million to build an extra room for the victim's families,' and I [said], 'No, we're not going to waste the state's money,'" said Ms. Petty. "'You guys have prison guards. You house death row inmates. If you can't handle six victim's family members in a room with the media, then you guys have a problem.'"

Signed by the governor in 2015, the law allows up to six family members to witness the execution from an adjacent room, and up to 12 to watch from a private room hooked up to a secure satellite feed.

The national attention on the now seven executions has reminded her how victims' families are treated, she said, often ignored or accused of being "just out for revenge."

"I would tell people to please take a moment to look at the victims and their stories, because their lives were stolen," Ms. Petty said. "Please take a moment to remember them. That's how I would conclude."

Representative Rebecca Petty presenting "Andi's Law," to the Arkansas House of Representatives.

Senator Bart Hester, Governor Asa Hutchinson, and Representative Rebecca Petty During the bill signing of Arkansas' "Andi's Law."

Governor Asa Hutchinson and the Senate and House co-sponsors of "Andi's Law."

EPILOGUE
2023

Twenty-four years have passed since I last saw your face, held your hand, and heard your voice. So much has changed. I have changed. If I could be granted one wish, it would be to sit across the dinner table from you in a seat that has been empty all these years, your seat, and tell you I love you. I have tried to envision the conversation I would have with you and the things I would say. It's hard because I now have trouble remembering what your voice sounded like; I only have a few videos where you are speaking. I'm sure your voice would now be that of a woman. I probably wouldn't know you if I passed you on the street, and that is a cruel realization. You will forever be that gentle 12-year-old apparition.

Though maybe I would say it's so good to see you. I have missed you every single day you've been gone. Not one day has passed that I haven't thought about you. It's been far too long.

No, it would be deeper than that. There would be tears,

weeping. I think the dam that has clogged my broken heart would burst open, and I would begin to feel something again. I have a hard time feeling anything. I feel alone in this world sometimes, like an oddity, but I know many people feel this same burden of grief and heartache. Anyone who has lost a loved one, particularly a child. I would convince them they are not alone.

Grief has been a long, lonely road. And even I am uncomfortable around those who have lost a loved one, strange as that seems. My wish is that mothers, fathers, grandparents, aunts, uncles, sisters, brothers, cousins, and loved ones who read this will realize they are not alone. At twenty-four years, I feel I am an old pro. Grief is cruel, but it proves the very existence of love. And love is the most important thing of all. Andi, I'm so sorry this happened to you. I hope you can forgive me for not being there to protect you from the predatory monster who took you away from us all. I have spent my life trying to right this wrong.

As for Karl Roberts, he is still sitting on death row, sucking away taxpayer dollars while bleeding hearts fight for his survival. He did have a major stroke about a year ago, and I don't know much more than that, except it must be a miserable existence to be in that 8 by 8 cell never seeing the light of day and being ill. I wonder if he wishes he would have let them execute him in 2004 when they tried. I have had no communication with him since his letter to me all those years ago, and for that I am glad. I have nothing to say to him, and I try not to think about him. I have concluded that Karl Roberts will, more than likely, just die in prison. He probably won't be executed because of today's political climate. The one good thing is he will never harm another child. His days are numbered. Sometimes, he creeps into my mind. Sometimes, awful dreams still come, and I have accepted they probably always will.

But, for the most part, I try to think of the good you brought to the world in your twelve short years. Because of you and your legacy, many laws have been changed to better this world. Laws protecting children, helping law enforcement, and crime victims. I am proud, not of myself, but of knowing that this has been carried out in your name, in your memory. Maybe this would have been your calling. However, for some reason, this mantle was passed to me, and I have been honored to carry it. I try my best to make the world a better place, as I believe you did. I want you to look down from heaven and be proud of me. I will never forget how silly, smart, giggly, and big your heart was. I know you are with God, and you walk with Jesus, and that brings me comfort.

So, I imagine sitting across from you at this table, looking into your eyes, holding your hands, and I wish to say thank you. Thank you for your love, thank you for the fire you ignited in me to not let one child who has suffered the ails of predators be forgotten. Your memory has encouraged me to fight for the most vulnerable, innocent little ones.

As I said before it is true that God gives beauty for ashes. Wipes our tears away. Redeems us, gives us eternal life if we believe. This has been the most meaningful lesson I have learned in all this.

I realize the world can be a very scary place but because you were here for a short time you brought hope, you brought peace, and you brought smiles to those who were facing hopelessness. You taught me the world can be an evil place, but you also taught me it is only black and dark if we let it be. So, shine bright little one.

You will always be my radiant light. I will see you again, I promise.

REFERENCES

CNN, B.C. (2004, January 6). *CNN.com - Arkansas executes mentally ill inmate - Jan. 7, 2004.*

https://www.cnn.com/2004/LAW/01/06/arkansas.executions/index.html

CNN Student News - *Bush signs law encouraging national Amber Alert system - April 30, 2003.* (2003, April 30).

https://www.cnn.com/2003/fyi/news/04/30/bush.amber/

Harris, T. (1988). *The Silence of the Lambs.* New York: St. Martin's Press.

King, S. (2000). *The Green Mile.* New York: Scribner.

Richardson, V. (2017, April 12). *Rebecca Petty, Arkansas lawmaker whose daughter was murdered, sees executions as end of long wait.* The Washington Times.

https://www.washingtontimes.com/news/2017/apr/12/rebecca-petty-arkansas-lawmaker-whose-daughter-was/